# *Bullock*

## *Chronicles of Deprivation and Despair in an American Prison*

*by Matthew Vernon Whalan*

*Foreword by Eddie Burkhalter*

KER
SPL
EDE
DEB
2025

Bullock: Chronicles of Deprivation
and Despair in an American Prison
ISBN 978-1-989701-45-4
First printing

Kersplebedeb can be contacted at:
                    Kersplebedeb
                    CP 63560
                    CCCP Van Horne
                    Montreal, Quebec
                    Canada
                    H3W 3H8
or email info@kersplebedeb.com

Visit the Kersplebedeb website at kersplebedeb.com or
order books from leftwingbooks.net

Cover art by Nikki "Kiki" Sanchez

For Jack Lahr and Natalya Mishin

But it is safe to assume that while a small prison is not certain to be successful, a large one is sure to be unsuccessful.

—Norman Johnston, *The Human Cage: A Brief History of Prison Architecture* (1973)

# Contents

# Foreword

There's a certain kind of silence in Alabama's prisons. It isn't peace. It's resignation. It's the dull, endless quiet of men waiting for someone to care. For decades, no one has—not in the ways that matter. Matthew Vernon Whalan's book is a rebuke of that silence, and to the system that has sustained it.

Reading this book I'm reminded of something that every journalist who's ever covered Alabama's broken prisons learns fast: time stands still in these places. Yes, the numbers get worse. The buildings crumble further. The drugs flow faster. The violence climbs higher. But the core problem is unchanged. Alabama continues to cage people in conditions the courts once called cruel and unusual—and still would, if they'd take another honest look.

Whalan doesn't write in abstractions. He's tracing a very real, very bloody line from the courtroom orders of the 1970s, to the body count we're now seeing. The problems the courts identified back then—overcrowding, lack of classification, rampant violence, indifference to mental illness—are not just present today. They're metastasized.

Whalan examines the everyday living conditions of those ensnared in these inhumane conditions, lending a voice to those who have been silenced. He is not pretending to present a finished analysis or explanation of how these tragic realities are tied

1

to so many others, which they most certainly are. Rather, this is a tightly focused and collectively narrated—using the words of the prisoners themselves—case study in neglect and dehumanization.

At the same time, it must be said, it is impossible to talk about the criminal justice system in Alabama without recognizing racial disparities in every aspect, from the makeup of the state's elected leaders and courthouses to its overpopulated jails and prisons.

Black Alabamians were over four times as likely as white Alabamians to be arrested for marijuana possession, even though the two groups use marijuana at roughly the same rate. In seven Alabama jurisdictions, the arrest disparity was more than 10 to 1.

Alabama's population is a little over a quarter Black, but more than half the people in our jails and prisons are Black. In May 2025, Black Alabamians comprised 54 percent of the state's prison population, and the racial disparity continues in the state's parole statistics. Between Jan. 1, 2021 and July 31, 2021 the Alabama Board of Pardons and Paroles denied parole for 77 percent of parole eligible white applicants but denied parole for 90 percent of Black applicants.

Perhaps it's little surprise that, given those stark racial disparities, things are much the same among the state's decision-makers. No Black person holds an elected statewide office in Alabama. White judges account for 154 of 192 elected circuit and district judges statewide, or 80 percent, despite whites making up 61 percent of the state's population (2020 U.S. Census).

Of the 38 Black judges statewide, 22 are in Jefferson County, leaving just 16 Black judges across the remaining 61 counties. All judges on the Alabama Supreme Court, the Court of Criminal Appeals, the Court of Civil Appeals and the director of the Alabama Office of Courts are white. Just three of Alabama's 41

Judicial Circuits are served by Black district attorneys, and 55 of 67 Alabama sheriffs are white. All judges on the Alabama Supreme Court, the Court of Criminal Appeals, the Court of Civil Appeals and the director of the Alabama Office of Courts, are white.

The result is that, like other U.S. states, Black people are disproportionately likely to be incarcerated in Alabama. While Black people make up 26% of Alabama's resident population, Black Alabamians constitute just over twice that proportion—53%—of those incarcerated in its prisons. If this discrepancy appears less stark than that of many other U.S. states, this must be seen as a perverse result of the fact that Alabama, like many other Southern states, incarcerates a significantly higher proportion of its population. According to the Prison Policy Initiative, almost 1% of Alabama's population are held in some kind of incarceration, be it jail or prison.

I've reported on Alabama's prison system for years, and what I've seen—what Whalan lays out clearly—is not a broken system. It's a system working as it was designed. A system built to discard lives. Alabama's prisons have always been about punishment, not rehabilitation or redemption.

Whalan listened to these men who live in these horrors, and his book demands a reckoning. It forces readers to confront the shameful truth: that Alabama has had every opportunity to change and has chosen, time and again, not to. That we are closing the books on preventable deaths—hundreds of them each year—and calling that "justice."

Matthew Vernon Whalan is doing what far too few have dared to do: drawing the through-line between what was and what is. He reminds us that history, especially here, is not past.

It is prologue. It is policy. And it is people—incarcerated people and the communities they come from—who pay the price.

Read this book. Then ask yourself why we let this happen. Again.

Eddie Burkhalter
Alabama Appleseed Center for Law and Justice
Piedmont, Alabama
June 2025

# Acknowledgements

Thanks so much to all who supported me on this project. Thanks to Nikki Sanchez, Coco Rhum, Jon Rosen, John Sheehy, Brody Lipton, Jason Myles, Beth Shelburne, "DC", Joshua Frank, and Ross Ion Coyle, for your help and/or various forms of encouragement on these stories. Thanks to Ben Burgis for convincing me at 1:00 in the morning not to self-publish this book. Thanks to Karl Kersplebedeb for taking an interest in the book and being a fine editor as well. I'd also like to thank the family, friends, and other loved ones, named and not, here and gone, who have supported me (or put up with me) over the years. To name a few: Gabriel Weiss, Miranda Neizer, Zachary Wigham, Karli Schrade, Daniel Guerra, Brendan Houlihan, Roland Obedin-Schwartz, Jimmy Davis Jr., Michael Rosenthal, Lynette Rummel, Adam Franklin-Lyons, Eoin Higgins, Jennifer Hunt, Jennifer Bidwell. Extra special thanks to my parents, John Whalan and Ellen Lahr, and my brothers Adam Whalan, Jackson Whalan, and Franklyn Davis. Finally, a deep thank you to all the prisoners in Alabama who have shared their stories and their time with me.

# Chapter 1
## "Homicidal and Suicidal"

BULLOCK PRISON IN UNION SPRINGS, Alabama opened in 1987 and is designed to hold 919 prisoners.[1] As of this writing in December 2024, the Alabama Department of Corrections (ADOC) has the number of people imprisoned there at 1,512.[2] Alabama prisons are currently, and consistently, at around 170 percent of capacity.[3]

Starting in November 2024, multiple prisoners from Bullock reach out to me to do interviews about the prison conditions and their lives. Those stories, assembled from late 2024 into 2025, comprise the bulk of this book. The names of those still imprisoned have been changed to protect their privacy.

* * *

In late November, I connect with a prisoner who I'll call "Derek." He's in his early 50s. He discusses his time incarcerated, struggles with physical and mental health issues, barriers to getting help, overcrowding, violence, being targeted as gay due to his recent HIV diagnosis, and many other topics. On and off, he has spent over 20 years of his life in prison. He's been serving his current sentence since 2006 and has been transferred through several prisons in the state during that time, as most prisoners in Alabama are.[4] All of his charges are for nonviolent crimes, mainly drug related.

Derek was diagnosed with HIV in recent years, which has caused him concern for his safety and has resulted in harassment and assaults from some of the other prisoners. In the past, he has also sustained knee and hip injuries, had surgery for both, and currently has an injured shoulder from falling in the midst of a seizure.

The seizures are one of several health issues, like hepatitis C and HIV, that "I didn't have before I got to prison, and now I have them," he says. His health issues also make him feel less able to defend himself than he used to be. Derek contracted HIV and hepatitis C from intravenous drug use but has been labeled a "ho" and "gay" by some other prisoners since he received the diagnosis.

When he was diagnosed with HIV, he reflects, "I came down and let the guys know in my dorm, so they could go get checked. I was trying to do that from the heart, but I have ... A couple times now, I wished I hadn't done that, because, like I said, it changed a lot of things for me in here. And it's got some of these guys looking at me sideways like, 'Damn, is this guy gay or not?' Because 'gay' is a rough thing in prison, man. For the most part, dudes that are gay, they get treated pretty rough. You're not allowed to go in the ice coolers and things like that. Certain things, they can't do, or they get their head knocked off in here."

As noted by *The Washington Post*, Federal authorities have "faulted [Alabama] state officials for what they said was a failure to fully investigate sex assaults in prison" and for "implying that a gay man cannot be raped."[5]

Derek continues, "I didn't want that kind of name put on me, but that's neither here nor there. And I done what I thought I had to do" by informing others of his condition. Derek explains that in any case there are other reasons people know of his diagnosis. He says prisoners are being denied privacy rights around certain medical information, which we'll come back to later in this story.

"The prison is flooded with HIV," he says, and, "It's not from homosexuality. It's from drug use."

*AL.com* reported in 2023, citing the Prison Policy Initiative, that "Alabama prison inmates are about three times as likely as other residents to have HIV."[6]

People labeled gay in prison are more likely to be assaulted, says Derek, and he repeatedly makes sure I understand throughout the conversation that he is not gay himself but is being mistreated just the same because of the connotations of his diagnosis.

"That's why I'm in the predicament that I am in," he says. "Like I told you, I can't protect myself right now," due to the shoulder injury, "and they know this. What would I do if they jump me right now? There would be nothing I could do. It wouldn't even take one good lick to that shoulder, and it'd be rough. It'd be over with for me. I can barely move the damn thing now. It hurts to even cough."

He's been assaulted recently, slapped in the face by a prisoner a couple of days before our interview. "It wasn't that bad, but if I'd tried to fight back or something, they do a lot of cludging in here. There are a lot of groups that run together, and if you jump on one, you've got to jump on all of them, that type of deal.

"And they know that I'm HIV positive. And that makes it even worse for me because they don't want to put their hands on me. So, if I do get attacked, for the most part, they'll attack me with weapons, sticks and stuff, to keep them from getting my blood on their hands and stuff."

Elaborating on the health issues and the violence, "The head trauma and the seizures is one thing," says Derek. "That was the first thing, basically. All the head traumas that I've been through were making me have these seizures ... Also, four of my teeth got knocked out at Staton due to being hit in the mouth with a lock. This is years ago.

"When this happened, I went back to the gate. And see, at Staton, you've got Staton, Elmore, and one other camp, all three of them right there together, and they all use the HCU, the Hospital Care Unit. So, I'm standing there bleeding, blood all over me, with my teeth in my hands, and [the officer] told me to go back, 'Go back.' I mean, scared and smashed like I was in the face with this lock, I'm not trying to go back to the dude that just beat me with this damn lock, standing down there. 'I'm not going that way.' How crazy would that be? He knocked four of my teeth out.

"Well, [the guard] wouldn't open the gate and let me go to the HCU. He was telling me to go back. I wasn't trying to disrespect the officer, or not obey his orders, but, to me, I couldn't see me going back, the way this dude was that just beat me with this lock.

"But, anyway, to make a long story short: Then the police came out there, and they jumped on me. And that got I&I involved in it, which is the Intelligence and Investigations Department of the ADOC, and that got them involved in it. A lady named Lieutenant Shepard that worked at the I&I came over there and talked to me and interviewed me. And by the next day, I was gone. They C-fifty-oned me."

(A C-51 is a transfer to another prison, often without cause, or not as punishment.)

"I wasn't in the next camp a full day—I hadn't healed yet—and that was when I got hit in the mouth again," he continues, "and that was when it broke my jaw and everything. I was at Ventress when that happened. Me and [another prisoner] was walking along together and then, next thing I know, he just planted one on me, hit me in the mouth. He hit me so hard it knocked me completely out. So, anyway, that was the one that broke my jaw that time. They said it fractured in 27 places.

"When I woke up, my mouth was wired shut. They were never supposed to wire my mouth shut to begin with because of me being a seizure patient, but they did. I ended up having to get surgery again and getting that other thing put on my face.

"The last time I got to see my mom alive was over at Ventress, before her and my sister both died of Covid in 2021. I was in the HCU at Ventress and she got to come see me one last time before they ended up dying. But, I had to see her like that, with that thing on my face, and it broke her heart.

"Anyway, whenever that happened, I ended up having to stay in the HCUs for a minute following that, back and forth between Kilby and Ventress, going to the doctors and stuff out there in the free world, and staying in those hospitals just trying to heal up."

Derek was "in a relationship with a woman in the free world for a long time. She rode with me for like 13 years," he says, but due to his imprisonment and the health issues that have come with it, Derek has let go of that relationship, too.

When he found out he was HIV positive, he "lost a lot of hope. Yes, I did," he recalls. "For a minute there, it had me thinking, 'I'm never going to get out of here.' And luckily, God and my spirit and the people in here were talking to me and saying, 'Derek, that's just a lie, man. That's just something that they want you to believe, because you can make it through this. You've made it this far. You could make it further.'

"But, I don't have much hope in this stuff anymore, and I let her go. I called her and I told her what the deal was [with the HIV diagnosis], and I told her even if I was to be out of prison, out on parole or something, I can't be with her. I can't go with her and be with her and take the chance of giving her this mess. Do you understand what I'm saying? So, I went ahead and told her, and told her that she should go on and go about her business if that's what she wanted to do, because I know she wants to have a life too, and I'm not trying to hold her back ... I have talked to her. She still answers the phone for me occasionally."

* * *

We again return to the topics of violence, health problems, and medical care in prison. I ask Derek more about his seizures.

"Head trauma," he reiterates. "And they've had to change up my seizure medications a couple of times. They had me on Depakote. Now I'm allergic to Depakote and I can't take that. So, they got me on a medicine called Keppra and I have to take it twice a day. 8:00 in the morning and 8:00 at night, they have pill calls. I get two big pills at morning and nighttime pill calls. I mean, I hate to say it, man, but I have to have that medicine, because if I don't take it, if I miss it one night, before I go down there to get my medicine again the next morning, I'll have a seizure."

Derek had his first seizure in 2009 or 2010, "after I had been hurt a few times" in the prison, he says.

"And then when I got hit over the head with that lock in Staton, it knocked my teeth out," he adds. "I don't know if you've ever been in any fights or anything before, but I've been in a lot of them in here, and I've gotten my brains beat in a lot of times, because of the cludging thing that I was telling you about. They're bad about that in here."

"Cludging" refers to prisoners ganging up to participate in assaults together, rather than one-on-one fights. It seems to be regional slang. I can find it defined or discussed only in court files, and only in this region.[7]

"Also, for the most part," he continues, "a lot of things that have happened to me have been caused by inmates, me getting assaulted by other inmates, yes, but some of the things that have happened to me have been caused by the police."

He gives an example he is struggling with now: "If I go and tell them that I'm homicidal and suicidal, they're supposed to lock me up. I tried to do that a few times, and they won't lock me up. They say that I'm faking it. They won't lock me up. And when I said I'm suicidal and homicidal, a lot of those times, I'm not just suicidal and thinking about taking my own life. I really am homicidal, man, because I'm tired of taking this shit I've had to take ... A lot of these things in here, especially in these last few years, I've just had to take, because I knew it was better to just take that than what it was going to be when I was going to try to fight back."

When he has seizures, he often doesn't remember what happened. "When my hip and my knee got broken," he recalls, "I was having a seizure. The inmates were banging on the window, trying to get the police's attention, because we're really overcrowded and they don't have enough people there. They don't have enough guards working here. In other words, they have guards working in the hallways and in cubes. Here recently, they haven't had enough guards to work the cubes. So, the guard in the hallway has to go in the cube and man the cube and open up our doors from inside the cube. Then they come back out in the hallway and run the hallway."

After the prisoners started banging on the windows when Derek was having a seizure, "They came down here to see what was going on," says Derek, "and the people in the dorm were telling [the officers] that I have seizures and stuff. And the lieutenant was coming up there thinking that I was wigging out on dope, and the inmates that they will listen to were telling him, 'Nah, man, that dude has seizures.' They told him, 'Don't walk up on him, man. Don't walk up on that dude. He's going to kick the shit out of you.'

"They're telling the lieutenant this. I'm over there, having a seizure. I don't know what's going on. But, obviously, I did kick him, but I don't know what I'm doing, and when they tried to hold me down or submit me or whatever, I go to ... kicking and stuff. Well, I kicked him. And he picked me up over his head and boomed me down on this damn concrete floor, and broke my hip and my knee, and they had to rush me out to the free world and I had to have hip surgery and knee surgery.

"And when I came back ... If they think that something has happened to you—and they've done the body charts on me and my head is busted and I can't tell them what happened and they don't know if I've gotten into a fight or what—they're supposed to protect me, man. But they don't. They just send me right back up to the same dorm.

"If I have a seizure in the dorm and they do get the police's attention, then they rush me up to the Hospital Care Unit. I wake up handcuffed, shackled, and belly-chained to the bed up there in the Hospital Care Unit. And most of the time, I've usually urinated on myself or something like that, because I'm straining so hard and seizing out so bad, and I'm begging these people to let me out of these handcuffs and shackles and stuff. I'm all cut up from the straining by it, because they say they have to put me in that because I'm kicking and stuff so hard. But shouldn't they have, like, straps with Velcro and stuff on them instead of putting you in handcuffs and shackles and stuff? But they don't, sir.

"This has gotten to the point where I've even told the inmates in the dorm, 'Man, look, if I'm not seizing out that bad, just don't even take me up there to healthcare.' They're like, 'Man, we've got to get the police and help you up there.' I was like, 'Dude, you don't understand, man.' I said, 'Every time I wake up there, I'm handcuffed and shackled and belly-chained to this damn bed. And it hurts. And I'd rather you just not even do that. If you can and I'm coming out of it and there's a way you can just put me on my bed, I'd rather you just put me on my bed than take me to the HCU."

\* \* \*

Derek also says the prison is flooded with fentanyl and other drugs. Asked how it's getting in, he reiterates what most prisoners and experts say: "It beats me, because we don't have any [prisoners] going out [into the free world] to work, so there's nobody going outside of the gates. So, if it's getting in here, it's got to be getting in here by the guards. It's a big business, man."

He says that when prisoners overdose, sometimes multiple prisoners a day, "They're wheeling them up [to the medical ward] in a laundry cart, in wheelchairs and stuff like that, because they don't have any gurneys to take people up there.

"They had the camp on lockdown for one or two days last week because they had like six or seven guys—bang, bang, bang, bang, bang, bang, bang—drug overdose, drug overdose, drug overdose, drug overdose, all back to back. They were rushing them up there … It's really bad here, man."

There are also "a lot of dudes in here getting amputated," says Derek. "Dudes I've been knowing for years, all over the system together, different camps together, they were fine last time I seen them and then I see them at this camp two or three years later, and his leg is gone, or I see another dude a couple years later and his foot is gone. I see another guy at a different camp and his fingers are gone."

Asked what the amputations are for, Derek answers, "All different types of stuff."

Indeed, amputations in Alabama prisons have been reported widely and the state has been sued in the past on this issue.[8]

Derek describes Bullock in greater detail. "Bullock, for one, is a mental institution," he says. "They have the main camp, which is where I'm at, and they have what they call the Blue Building, which is for the real bad mental [illness], like talking to themselves and stuff like that. If people want to kill themselves or stuff like that, that's where they put them.

"Except, when you go in to report that you're homicidal or suicidal, they're supposed to lock you up, but they won't with me, and I've tried to tell them that it ain't just suicidal. I'm homicidal. It's hard taking this shit. I'm getting to the point where it's like …

Like I said, I was raised by a man ... My dad wasn't no sissy ... And I can hear his voice in my head, and he's like, 'Man, will you keep taking this shit?'

"Look, it's a bad situation when you get to a point where you really feel like you're not going to ever get out of prison. And there's dudes in here that got three, four life sentences, running wild with each other, and they know they're never getting out of prison. And they don't give a shit. They don't care about the police. They damn sure don't care about other inmates. They will kill you. I thought that after them finding out I had HIV it would ... But, there's still guys that want to have sex with me. They still talk about stuff like that. It's crazy."

Derek returns to the privacy issues surrounding healthcare in the prison. In theory, prisoners have HIPPA rights. In my research, I also found that Alabama Department of Corrections' Administrative Regulation Number 604, dated March 8, 2024, Section III reads, "Confidentiality: Provision or documentation of services in a manner such that Protected Health Information cannot be overheard or otherwise accessed by unauthorized persons."[9]

In practice, it's a different story. As Derek explains, "The prison system makes it so easy for [other prisoners] to find out about it anyway. We do these telemonitor things, where you have to go see the doctor on the telemonitor. And the guy that we see is a doctor out of Atlanta ... And everybody in the prison that sees this particular doctor has HIV ... They make it so easy for the other inmates in this camp to find out who it is that's got [HIV] because they do a newsletter every day, and that newsletter has got your appointments, the appointments for the camp on there for the next day. It's got everybody's name, AIS number, bed number, dorm number, if they've got to go to the HCU, or classifications. And everybody that goes and sees this particular doctor ... that I was telling you about from Atlanta, on that telemonitor, he's the only doctor for the HIV, so they know that everybody that goes and sees him is HIV positive.

"So, if somebody did want to keep that private, because it is our right to keep our medical issues private ... We do not have to share that with other people if we don't want to, but it's so easy for them to find out that people are going to find out anyway ... Since a lot of these people have found that out about me—and like I said, it changed their view of me—they were looking at me like a homosexual for it ... but I'm not."

He reiterates the frustration and rage building up as a result of the harassment from other prisoners, worsened by his health issues and limited ability to defend himself.

"I know that even though I'm in this bad health and stuff like I am, even with my shoulder like it is right now, I could do something to make them stop this shit. If they're going to beat the shit out of me or whatever is going to happen ... I can tell you one damn thing: If I wanted to, I can put a stop to it. That's why I'm trying to tell [the officers] that I'm homicidal, man, because I am homicidal right now, especially when it comes down to these people slapping me and me having to taking this shit from them, treating me any kind of way.

"And when I go try to get the police to lock me up to keep from getting in trouble and getting another disciplinary, or catching not just a disciplinary but a case ... Man, I already have a problem of getting out of here on this life sentence for [drug] trafficking. What you think they're going to do if I stab one of these dudes in here and catch a murder case or something because I was rightfully trying to protect myself? I'm telling these people. I'm telling them I need to be locked up, to put me in protective custody, and they will not do it."

* * *

Later, Derek discusses the overcrowding and violence problems in Bullock, consistent with prisons throughout the state, and which cause and exacerbate many other problems, if not all the other problems.

"Man, it is super crowded in here," he says. "Being homeless in the first place is a bad situation, but being homeless in prison, that's even more terrible. And these dudes are having to sleep on the floor, and they don't have a mat, and they don't have any blankets...

"I see these older men in wheelchairs and stuff like that. These guys wheel them to the chow hall and they're just taking their food from them, man. So, a lot of dudes don't get to eat. They're hungry.

"I'm looking at a dude right now. He's laying on the floor, concrete floor. He does not have a mat. He does not have a blanket, a sheet, or nothing, just his clothes, and he doesn't have a coat. I'm looking at him, watching him right now. He's got his arms pulled inside his shirt ... He has to have his arms pulled inside his shirt because he's freezing, laying there on this damn floor, and the police know it and they won't do anything about it.

"Well, the police might give you a mat. You take that and put it on your bed, and the first time they call you out to chow hall or something like that, you come back and it's gone. Somebody done stole the damn thing. What are you supposed to do about it?

"That's one of those situations where I've closed up from fighting, man. I didn't used to have to take this kind of stuff. I'm not used to that. I've had to draw back into myself and take that kind of stuff.

"But, I'm telling you, Matthew, I'm super homicidal right now, and if I do something or hurt one of these dudes, man, I can't get myself out of here. But, if I'm going to be stuck in here, I'd rather be in lockup. I'd rather be getting some help to where I at least have some kind of protection. The officers don't understand that. Man, they've got to put me in that cell...

"I've done that one time here. About seven or eight months ago, I stabbed a dude. Me and him got into it and I stabbed him, and when the police came to find out what was going on, they ran out here. They know me by name. So, they're like, 'Derek, what the hell you got going on?' I was like, 'I don't know, man.' He said, 'Who you fighting with?' I was like, 'I don't know who they were. I only know one dude...' And I said, 'I don't know anything about anybody else, but I know about this one dude...' And the officer was like, 'What do you mean?' And I still had the ice pick in my hand. I held it out to him and I said, 'I stabbed him,' and I held the ice pick out to him and tried to give it to him. And you know what he told me? He said, 'I don't want that shit, man. Throw that down.' And then I threw it down on the yard and he didn't even take the darn thing, didn't even write me up for it ... I guess it wasn't bad enough for them. They're not trying to do no paperwork, man. They're already low on officers, and they're not trying to do no paperwork."

# Chapter 2
## "A Crying Shame"

"JORDAN" HAS BEEN INCARCERATED in Alabama for well over two decades, in Bullock for over 15 years.

He tells me Bullock is in part meant to be a mental health facility, confirming what Derek said in Chapter 1, but that prisoners with and without mental health issues are all mixed up together and prisoners with mental health issues are often targeted, taken advantage of, and assaulted.

"A lot of these guys, they came from the streets with mental health issues and problems like that, and a lot of the guys they got down here mixed up with these mental illness guys—mental health issues for real—they're extorting these guys [who have mental health issues], conniving these guys, bullying these guys, and these guys is real slow ... A lot of these guys need to be moved up out of this dorm, man, out of this mental health dorm," says Jordan.

"There's a lot of bullying going on down here," he says, and reiterates that it's "guys with mental health issues" who are the primary targets of the bullying, adding, "They're manipulating them, taking their shit," and "making them do things that they shouldn't do."

Jordan says a lot of the prisoners with mental health issues are the older ones who have been in the longest. "They go 20 something years, 30 something years. It's mental health, man, for real ... Matt, we've been gone 20 something years, man, and these guys just got to prison, man, and they think they've got the ups on us because we've been gone so long, 20, 30 years, and they're just bullying us ... Something need to be did about it. I'm tired of it, tired of it, tired of it ... They be bullying these guys, beating these guys, slamming these guys. All they've got to do is roll that camera. They've got a camera down here in these dorms, man."

Jordan has been keeping notes on the dates and times of different violent incidents in the prison.

He goes on to discuss the sanitary conditions in Bullock, as well as problems with the infrastructure of the building itself.

"This prison down here in Union Springs, that kitchen down there, they got their damn septic tank built up out of this kitchen," he says. "When we go eat down there, man, you can smell the goddamn septic tank. It stinks so bad in the kitchen, you can taste it in the food when you eat it, man. You can't even eat the food, man. It is crazy around here. The septic is down there by the kitchen, and the septic tank smells so bad, when you go to eat, you can taste the smell in the food."

He adds that someone "needs to come down here and inspect and do something about this shit."

Another problem in Bullock, says Jordan, is that "the water is running into the prison when it rains."

In a statement in which the near allegory is apparently unintended but nonetheless wasn't lost on me, he adds, "The foundation of the prison system done sunk. The prisons are sunk. So, the ground is higher than the foundation."

Many other inmates and journalists over the years have exposed video accounts of the flooding problem in Bullock Prison.[10] I've documented similar issues in Fountain Prison and elsewhere.

Jordan continues, "So, you can't do nothing about rain ... When it's raining, it's running dead in the door, running on the ground. We've got blankets. They got blue blankets, what we use to cover up with. They gave us 100 blue blankets to put up out their doors, man. All in the gym, washing, running in the doors, man, all in the kitchen, all in the prison, water just spraying in. It's been raining for the last three days. It's getting inside the dorm, man. The dorm is flooded. And the sewage system is backing up through the drain system, man, and they walk all over the floor and walk all through the sewage waters. They track it all over the dorm, man."

He adds, "There's feces, man. You've got guys down here shitting all over the place inside the dorm, urinating themselves, bleeding on themselves, and they should be in the infirmary, man," or in the medical ward "down there at Kilby."

Indeed, if the prisons weren't so overcrowded, perhaps they would be getting medical attention more quickly, or would be in a medical ward. Although, then again, perhaps not.

"Guys are real sick, man. These guys got medical issues," says Jordan.

There are also "so many rats and roaches down here, it's a crying shame," he says. As I've reported many times elsewhere, Alabama prisons are full of rats and cockroaches, along with other creatures sometimes as well.[11]

"We tell them all the time to spray this place. It's infested with rats and roaches," Jordan continues. "It's infested. [My] dorm needs to be sprayed, man. There's a million roaches in here ... Turn the lights off and roaches go running everywhere."

He says the rat problem in Bullock has improved slightly in recent years, primarily based on his observation that the rats seem to have gotten smaller. He recalls they "used to come out of the woods" and "some were 12 inches long."

Jordan touches on the overcrowding problem in prison as well.

"It's way overcrowded. They've got guys sleeping on the floor, guys in the wrong dorm, guys trying to get out, running from the other dorms, got guys beating them up ... That's what a lot of it is. These guys are getting beat up, manipulated and beat up ... That's what's going on in the prison system, and that's been going on a long, long time," he says, adding that he also thinks the prisons need more officers.

He says the overcrowding problem is so bad that prisoners "can't even get on their assigned beds."

Jordan sees many of the same health issues in the prison that Derek described in Chapter 1, including amputations.

"Bullock is supposed to be a mental health facility," he explains, "like for people who went crazy that have mental health issues, like people [who] talk all night to their self, peeing on their self, can't walk, diabetes. Somebody got limb issues or might got one leg, or might got no legs, some types of stuff like that, or might just can't walk, or might got a spinal issue, them types of issues. That's what we have down here in Union Springs: guys urinating on themselves, shitting on themselves."

There are over 80 prisoners in his dorm.

Prisoners with these various health issues, says Jordan, "should be in the infirmary, should be in a camp where [prisoners] have been diagnosed with these types of issues. Colostomy bags on their side and stuff, they should be in a camp where people just have [health problems] like that. They shouldn't be around regular inmates," especially "when they're having all these feces in the population."

The bathroom area of the prison is also "messed up," says Jordan. "They need to come and pressure wash these things, man. They've got holes all in the showers, water running all in the walls, busted pipes running through the walls. The water is constantly running, all the time, man."

He says many of the drains in the floor are no longer functional, and, "When it rains, you've got to push it in the shower, try to mop it up and push it in the shower ... They ain't got working drains in the floor no more. It's crazy, water just running all over the place. When it rains, I have to mop up for three hours, man. I shouldn't have to clean up like that."

He again says he believes the prison should be "condemned" and "shut down," and recalls that they "said they would shut it down" but never did.

A *WSFA-12* article from 2019 covered the possibility of Bullock Prison closing, focusing entirely on the impact on the town and local businesses and not saying anything about the prisoners inside, let alone including comments from any of them.[12]

Jordan elaborates on the subject of amputations: "They lost limbs, lost their toes, or their foot, because of the sugar. And [for] wheelchairs, there ain't ramps that go in and out of the doors. The doors will open up for the wheelchair to go through and you can hardly get through the damn door," he says.

Jordan suspects a lot of the amputations are from diabetes, but he also knows prisoners who "say they ain't diabetic, but they got their damn leg cut off, and their toes and foot. They say they ain't no diabetic but they sure got their limbs cut off."

Jordan adds that drugs are a major problem in prison. "The police are corrupt, man," he says. "The police, they're bringing all the dope into this damn place. That's who is doing it ... That's how they're getting it, because there ain't nobody else leaving here. Who else leaves this prison? Nobody else. How you think it's getting in here?"

And he says the drugs, combined with the overcrowding, are another main driver of the violence.

In addition to prisoners with mental health issues, "There's a lot of older guys in here getting beat up," says Jordan, and he believes the violence in the prison has grown worse over the years.

The ADOC and the prison administration "know the problem," says Jordan, "but they won't solve the problem."

# Chapter 3

## "Closest to Hell That You Can Get"

In December, I interview a third prisoner in Bullock about living conditions and his experiences doing time in Alabama. I'll call him "Tim." Tim has been doing time for around a decade and has recently taken up the challenge of writing a book about his life, under conditions very much not conducive to writing. He started working on it several months before our interview and is a few chapters in.

Having just come from chow hall before our conversation, Tim says the food in Bullock is "nasty," and, "You probably get about 12 or 13 bites" per meal.

He says the biggest problems in Alabama prisons are "overcrowding, lack of security, violence, extortion."

Extortions can happen "if you're not affiliated with organizations or something like that," meaning prison gangs. And if you have money on your books, "and others see this, well, they want that. So, it's either you pay, or you get beatings, or stabbed up."

Elaborating on the cramped conditions, Tim explains how "overcrowding brings the lack of security. They're supposed to have so many officers for so many inmates," but at least in the dorms he is in and near, "they have maybe one officer for two dorms, and they don't walk through" the dorm while patrolling, only when they do the count twice a day. Otherwise, "They just come up, look in the window, and walk off," says Tim.

Tim estimates that there are between "80 and 100 people" in his dorm "at any given time. This dorm is maybe 100 feet long by 40 feet wide ... If I lay flat on my rack, I can reach out with my left arm and touch the person that sleeps next to me. If I reach out with my right arm, I can touch the person that sleeps on the other side of me, which means we all have to share very small spaces."

Tim also says people are sleeping on the floor. There are many reasons people sleep on the floor, "usually because someone else wanted their rack, wanted their bed, and basically, in here, like I said, if you're not affiliated, you're either going to get cludged out or stabbed up or something like that, if you don't go along with whatever they want."

He believes there are more prisoners in his dorm than beds. He doesn't know if everyone in that dorm is assigned to it, "but they're in here." Often when officers come in to do the count, "there are people standing by the piss troughs and the phones."

I ask what the bathroom situation is like in Bullock. "This dorm here," says Tim, "we have four toilets in the entire dorm, two urinals for the entire dorm, and three shower stalls for the entire dorm. That's not much for 100 people."

Tim reiterates what other prisoners have said about drugs being a major problem in Bullock. In Bullock, there are "dope fiends, dope dealers, and people who try to stay out of the way."

In the past, he says, there were more trades and services that prisoners exchanged, and exchanged goods for, like fixing radios or tattoo art, and he believes many such trades still exist in other prisons. "But, those don't exist here, because everybody spends all their money on dope."

There are no more "radiomen, people who used to work on the radios, because nobody has a radio," he explains, adding that there are hardly even any cigarettes or coffee going around anymore.

Tim feels the drug problem in prison is "ridiculous. This year, I've seen four or five people dead. Overdoses." Prisoners "are being hit with Narcan on a regular basis."

"I'm sitting right here, looking around the dorm, and I can see at least five or six people smoking flakka, and maybe three smoking ice. And people I can't see are probably laid over, nodding out on fentanyl. It's real bad. It's really available."

Tim tells me he himself has struggled with addiction while doing time.

"At one point, I had a little problem with it," he says, "and I didn't like how it was turning out. So, it was hard, but I went cold turkey. I never was on the fentanyl or the flakka. My drug of choice was ice ... It was readily available. I was getting it for $40 a gram."

The hardest thing about quitting drugs in prison is that "there wasn't an escape anymore," Tim reflects. "It's an escape. That's the number one reason, I think, why people use in prison. It's an escape from this place ... This camp ... is the closest to hell that you can get."

He got through quitting by trying to sleep as much as possible, which is often not much, and not many hours in a row, a problem we'll return to later. But, "once a person makes up their mind, they make up their mind," he says, so he stuck with his recovery.

"I've been from the downside to the upside to out of the way," he continues. "At one point, I was a user, and I got tired of it. I cleaned myself up. And then I started dealing. And I got tired of the problems that come along with that. So, I just got out of the way."

When he was a dealer, Tim got his drugs from other prisoners and flipped them, explaining how those prisoners were getting their drugs from the guards, confirming what all other prisoners and experts in Alabama have told me. "There's only one set of people that leaves the prison every day and comes back in. So, it's not hard to figure out."

\* \* \*

Returning to the topic of overcrowding, Tim discusses the heat wave that swept over the country in the summer of 2024.

"Miserable, real miserable," he says, "because we're packed in here like sardines, so close and so tight. There's very little airflow. We don't have AC, nothing like that."

Asked if they had fans during the heat wave, "We had two fans for the entire dorm," he answers. "One fan at one end of the dorm and one fan at the other end of the dorm. It's miserable. And the heat like that, it causes people to be outside of their normal character, because when the heat is up like that, everybody is aggravated already, and the smallest things set people off."

\* \* \*

Tim knows one prisoner "with an actual hole into his neck," he tells me, when I ask what kinds of health issues he sees in prison. "You can see into his neck ... It's bad enough you can smell it." Another guy's "feet look like they have gangrene ... The smell is horrible."

Due to overcrowding, "Since everybody lives so close to each other, when one person catches a cold, everybody is going to catch it."

Like Derek in Chapter 1, Tim also says "thievery" is a major problem, including theft of beds.

"Every time you go to chow, you're leaving your bed unprotected," he explains, "your bed and all your stuff. There are so many people that come back from chow and their whole damn mat is missing, or somebody came in from another dorm and took their mat."

The mats that prisoners are provided with by the ADOC are "about an inch and a half, two inches thick, all like kindergarten mats. And people want two mats to sleep on. So, they'll either kind of buy mats from other people, or steal them ... I've bought a couple mats. I don't like these small [mats], so any time somebody comes through here trying to sell one, I'm going to buy it if somebody else doesn't beat me to it. But, because of that, that causes people to go out and steal mats, because they're like, 'Hey, I can go out and get somebody to buy a mat if I go get one.'"

He says the mats are "maybe two-and-a-half feet wide, maybe six feet long, like kindergartener mats."

During the Covid pandemic, Tim was in a quarantine dorm "for a long time" at Kilby Prison, which "sucks." In the quarantine dorm, "it's even more overcrowded than a regular dorm, and you have to stay on your bed pretty much all the time."

Tim recalls how he "worried a lot" during the pandemic, "worried about my family. Both my parents were in their 80s. My mother just passed, back in April [2024]." He has also seen outbreaks of scabies, lice, and plenty more in prison.

Losing his mother while he was in prison was "very, very painful ... I wasn't allowed to go to the funeral, or any viewing."

I've written elsewhere about the prohibitively expensive process of trying to attend a loved one's funeral for prisoners, and the added pain of dealing with the grief of losing a loved one who is in the free world while one is in prison.[13]

Tim also lost his brother in 2021, "and I wasn't allowed to go to his funeral or anything like that [either]. When you lose somebody in prison, it's very hard. I wasn't able to say bye. I wasn't able to get one last look. None of that."

For Tim, "Being out of my element and being away from my family" are the hardest aspects of being in prison, "And of course, loss of freedom. I don't think anyone deserves what people go through in an Alabama prison."

# Chapter 4: Plumbing Disasters Continue

CHRISTMAS EVE, I GET a call from Derek in Bullock, where plumbing and flooding disasters have continued in the days before. Unpaid prisoners, as per usual in Alabama and much of the country, are tasked with managing the mess themselves.

I'm out with family when Derek calls, so I don't have my recorder. I do it old school and write down as much of what he's saying as I can as fast as I can while he's talking, pausing here and there to clarify and make sure I'm keeping up with him.

All the floor drains in his dorm are "overflowing with shit and piss," says Derek. "Everything, shit, piss, overflowing into the dorm."

Many of the prison staff are "fitting to shut down for Christmas until the New Year," and prisoners are telling other prisoners "nobody can take a leak or take a crap and nobody can take a shower ... They're telling us not to flush the toilets."

Prisoners often make the rules as guards are hardly present in the Alabama system, and will be even less so as the holiday week begins. Many guards, medical staff, and others throughout the prison will not be at work. A small private security force that the ADOC has hired to work the cubes will be there, Derek explains, but otherwise, staffing will be low.

Normally, prisoners use their blankets to try to mop the water off the floor, but as I am interviewing Derek, there are two garbage cans in the dorm full of water. A loose garbage bag on the floor is now being used for garbage, "and that's going to fill up soon," he says.

The day before, Derek witnessed a prisoner assaulted by other prisoners for being unable to control his bowel movements and having an accident. Now they're telling each other no one can use the toilet.

* * *

The day after Christmas, Derek calls me again to follow up about the plumbing issues (toilets not flushing, sewage overflowing from the floor drains into the dorm, prisoners unable to shower, shit, or piss, and other problems).

I ask how things have been going the past couple of days. I have my recorder this time.

"Two mornings ago, when we came back from morning breakfast, chow hall—this is at like 3:00, 3:30 in the morning—me and Jordan started working when we came back from breakfast. And I know—I know, man—we worked for at least six hours straight, sweeping the water and stuff up off this damn floor," he recounts.

He and Jordan took it upon themselves to do anything they could to deal with the situation. The state won't help them fix the plumbing or clean up the mess. As for the other prisoners, "because of their mental health," says Derek, "some of them are incapable of doing it, but the ones who are [capable], some of them are just like, 'Nah, I'm not going to clean that shit up for the state.' They're like, 'Fuck the state. I'm not doing shit for the state.' But, if we don't do it, they're going to track through that shitty, pissy water, and track it all over the dorm. We're trying to keep it contained in just the bathroom area."

Derek continues, "So, Jordan and I had to take trash bags—and [a guard] did give us a pair of rubber gloves, thank God, but if they hadn't, we were going to do it with the trash bags anyway and just wash our hands—but we had to take trash bags in deep down into the shitters, like, take a trash bag and pop it open, and get the bottom of the trash bag in one hand and sort of open it up and feed it down your arm and then reach down into the toilet and get the hunks of shit and toilet paper and stuff out of there and throw it into a big trash bag.

"We had to clean all that shit out of those shitters in order to start trying to get that water to go down. And now, we got it [down] but still cannot flush the toilets, shitters, take a shower, nothing, without the water running up in the drains in the floors. They had to call Roto-Rooter type people out there, free world people, to come out. We got word through the ear from one of the maintenance men that works here that said the septic tanks that they have on the outside of the camp, out back right there, are overflooding, and they have to get [free world plumbers] to come out here and, I guess, pump some of that stuff out of those septic tanks.

"But, anyway, all that water and stuff that we were getting up, we were having to put it in those trash cans. Remember I told you we didn't have any trash cans right now because they were filled up with water? And a lot of that water had trash and stuff in it, pieces of shit, man, toilet paper and stuff like that. But, regardless, we had to drag those trash cans full of water—I mean, 50-gallon trash cans, man, things are heavy—we had to take and drag those out by the back door, by the shift office.

"The thing about it is what I'm telling you can all be proven, because they've got cameras, and we've got times and dates.

"We had to pull those trash cans out the backdoors, by the shift office, and pour that water out the back doors. So, all that water is standing out there now. It looks like a shit pond out there is what it looks like. I don't know if you live in a city or whatever, but we have shit ponds around here, down in the South, that people throw stuff like that into. It's around chicken plants and stuff like that.

"But, anyway, that's what it looks like out the back door of that shift office, man, and it's nasty. And it stinks in here so bad. We tried to get them to give us some bleach, and some other chemicals like Pine Sol and stuff like that, to try to help us clean up in here, so we can get rid of some of the smell, but they ain't give us any.

"We just had to clean the mop out as much as we could with good hot water, and wring it out as good as we could, and keep it cleaned up. And me and Jordan, we worked for six hours straight on Christmas Eve," early into Christmas morning.

Sometime between 2007 and 2009—he can't remember exactly—"I was at Easterling [Prison], and they had, not a riot, but a lockdown. 108 of us went out in the middle of the field during yard call, and when they called the lockdown to put us back into the dorms and everything, to close the yard down, we couldn't go back in. We stayed out there. And we stayed out there and then they brought in their riot team, their CERT team, all that. But there was 108 of us.

"Actually, they didn't have enough personnel to do anything with us if we had really wanted to buck. You know what I'm saying?

"So, the other day, when all this shit water was in here and we couldn't breathe in here and these people wouldn't open the doors, when they did open the doors, for pill call and stuff like that, a whole bunch of us started to get together and do that same thing.

"We were all going to just leave out of the dorm—and we were going to chow—but we were going to walk down the hallway, and we weren't going to walk back down until they've done something about this shit.

"That's the state of mind these guys are in, Matthew. And they are talking about doing that big time ever since they started talking about it the other night.

"I've been trying to keep up with this stuff for you, but right now, I know I counted 213. Now, think about that. Back when we did this [in Easterling], there was only 108 of us. You got 213 prison inmates go down the hallway and tell them, 'Fuck you. We ain't marching down until y'all do something about this shit,' and there's not going to be anything they can do about that. They're going to call in the riot team and the CERT team and all that shit."

# Chapter 5: Note on the Recent History of Bullock and the Alabama Prison System

FROM THE EARLY 1970s to the early 80s, there was a long, ultimately unsuccessful effort to reform the Alabama prison system in the federal courts, in a case presided over by Judge Frank Johnson and later by Judge Robert Varner. One of the central cases was *Pugh v. Locke* in 1976, in which Judge Johnson issued his January 13 court orders to the state to address the problems in Alabama's prison system.[14]

The orders related to overcrowding, segregation and isolation, classification of prisoners, mental health care, protection from violence, living conditions, food service, correspondence and visitation, vocational, work and recreational opportunities, physical facilities, and staff.

Today, the state's prisons are once again being challenged in the federal courts—issues like severe overcrowding, violence, poor healthcare, the absence of an effective classification system (or indeed any classification system), the state's inability to protect prisoners in its care, understaffing. Not to mention state officials' preference to address overcrowding and inhumane living conditions by simply building more prisons, this in spite of orders by Judges Johnson and Varner to not solve the problem that way.

These issues were not solved by that previous decade of

litigation, and Alabama's prisons are facing largely the same problems today. Indeed, the state's prison system is arguably worse now than it was then.

In Larry W. Yackle's *Reform and Regret*, the primary legal history of litigation in the 1970s and 80s against the Alabama prison system, Yackle points out the following:

> From the earliest days, and increasingly after the Civil War, the Alabama penal system was charged at once to pay for itself and to accommodate large numbers of inmates [...]. These two themes, the requirement of self-support and crowding, were ever in conflict; the attempt to reconcile them condemned the Alabama prison system to failure.[15]

This remains true today. Since the end of World War II, the forced labor of Alabama prisoners has increasingly been utilized to maintain the facilities in which the forced laborers are themselves imprisoned.

Recently, this tension between "self-support" and overcrowding played out in dramatic fashion, as Republican Governor Kay Ivey and the legislature scandalously diverted hundreds of millions of dollars in Covid Relief Funds to building new men's prisons. And the state plans to continue building more after those are done, partly to "address" overcrowding.[16] There are more than a few problems with that, but as it pertains to overcrowding specifically, one stands out: They are also closing four older prisons at the same time, because those prisons are dilapidated and can't be used anymore.[17]

To illustrate how Alabama's prison system in the 1970s and 80s compares with today (which is saying a lot, because it was bad enough then) and for an idea of how much progress, if any, has been made, we'll compare and contrast some of Yackle's descriptions of Alabama's prisons then with contemporary descriptions of the state's prison system today, including from Alabama journalist Eddie Burkhalter, now a researcher at Alabama Appleseed Center for Law & Justice, and one of the best reporters to have covered the prisons in recent years.

At one point in *Reform and Regret*, Yackle notes that a particularly bad stretch in the early 1970s brought more attention to the problems with Alabama prisons and added urgency to the legal challenges getting underway at that time:

> [T]he attention of prison authorities was diverted to even more serious difficulties within the system. The prison population had been growing for years, but now the influx of new inmates was staggering. Frustration and anger grew in geometric proportion. The result in Alabama was what it had been in Attica in New York only two years earlier. Through the long summer and fall of 1973, local newspapers carried scattered stories of inmate violence. Reports that inmates had been stabbed, raped, or murdered became common. By official count, a total of twenty-seven prisoners lost their lives in the Alabama penal system in the 1972–1973 period. Guards were also occasionally injured or killed. The rate of incidents promised to be higher still if the legislature enacted pending bills, sponsored by Attorney General Baxley, to increase prison sentences, and thus the number of inmates, dramatically.[18]

Compare what were considered to be particularly scandalous numbers in the early 70s to what we are seeing now. Take this report from December 2022, 50 years after the period Yackle was writing about:

> More people incarcerated in Alabama's prisons have died so far in 2022 than in any single year for decades. In the first 11 months of the year, 222 people have died in the state's prisons.
>
> The Alabama Department of Corrections had not reported the total number of deaths in 2022. Press have confirmed 222 deaths, which exceeds the toll recorded during the height of the Covid pandemic.[19]

Or consider this breakdown of more recent numbers by Burkhalter:

> Alabama prisons saw a record 325 deaths in 2023. Of those, 253 investigations have closed, and 112 deaths were preventable, with 10 homicides, 13 suicides and 89 overdose deaths. That per 100,000 homicide rate is four times the national rate, according to the FBI's most recent data.
>
> The Alabama overdose mortality rate in prisons last year of 435 per 100,000 was 20 times the national rate across state prisons, according to the latest available national data.
>
> From Jan. 1–June 20, there were 161 deaths among the incarcerated in Alabama prisons. (Data via records request) Last year we saw a record 325 deaths, and the year before a record 270. We could well set another record this year.[20]

As the litigation from the 1970s and 80s wound down and was ultimately abandoned, Alabama state officials leaned into passing harsher and harsher sentencing laws[21] and reducing pardons and paroles.[22] As mentioned above, they are now even using Covid Relief Funds to build new prisons.

Journalist Beth Shelburne has written about the current parole board's extremely high rejection rate, as well as its corrupting effects on the state's work-release programs.[23] In a phone interview, Eddie Burkhalter described the Alabama Board of Pardons and Paroles as an institution that "rips families apart ... rips communities apart."[24]

State officials in the early 80s constantly claimed that building new prisons, rather than changing the sentencing laws or fixing the problems in the prisons they already have, would address the problems of overcrowding, violence, and other issues— overcrowding being the main, most persistent issue, up to this day. Whatever extent to which the construction of new prisons addressed any of these problems was short-lived. New prisons rapidly filled up, became overcrowded once again, and were quickly showing signs of serious construction and design flaws, with open dormitory spaces that were supposed to be used for so-called "vocational" and other purposes instead being used to house prisoners.

This is the context in which Bullock Prison, St. Clair Prison, and others I've written about were opened, as the court cases against Alabama's prison system died down in the 80s, as the plaintiffs and the judges essentially gave up on trying to get Alabama state officials to cooperate. St. Clair in particular was built with promises of reducing overcrowding. Bullock Prison and others were built in the same context.

Over the years of doing this work, I've been struck by how many people, even prisoners themselves, assume that the physical structural issues of the buildings being so dilapidated are simply because they are so old. But St. Clair opened in 1983. Bullock opened in 1987. Donaldson opened in 1982. Ventress Prison in Clayton opened in 1990. Bibb Prison opened in just 1998. These are not particularly old buildings. Several of my sources have been in prison for longer than many of these facilities have existed.

Writing in the late 80s, just a few years after the prison litigation of that era had fizzled out, Yackle noted toward the end of his book, "Even the new prisons in the north showed signs of wear; in the south, the threat of slipping back to ruin was palpable."[25]

By the early 80s, the "average age of prisoners entering the system had dropped well below 30 years, posing the real possibility that Alabama's prisons might actually be asked to house individual prisoners for nearly half a century," Yackle wrote in 1989.[26] Many of my sources have been in prison for decades, longer than half their lives, longer than all of mine.

Indeed, state officials were aware at the time that the opening of St. Clair and other prisons would not address overcrowding, let alone the numerous other issues in the prisons.

In 1981, a federal judge asked commissioner Joseph Hopper "for the names of prisoners having less than one year to serve," and in December of that year, "ordered the release of 352 prisoners with 'good conduct records' who were scheduled for release within six months in any event."[27] Commissioner Hopper was vehemently opposed to the release order, and "a spokesperson in his office said that the judge was now reaching down to the 'scum' of the prison population and proposing early release for men who had committed violent felonies."[28] However, in an interview a few weeks later, Hopper conceded that crowding could not be eliminated by the construction of new facilities. Neither the planned prisons in St. Clair and Jefferson counties, nor a third in the Tennessee Valley, would keep pace with the growing population of inmates. On the contrary, according to the corrections department's own projections, the state would need a new prison capable of housing 1,000 prisoners every year through 1990 and beyond in order to achieve and maintain adequate space for prisoners [if they are going to achieve that by building new prisons]. Each such prison would cost $30 million to build and roughly $600 million to operate over its useful life. "When we really get down to economics," Hopper declared, "we cannot afford to lock up all these people."[29]

In 1983, Yackle notes, St. Clair was opened and put to the test of how much its new existence would help to address overcrowding in Alabama prisons. Days later, prisoners were "redistributed" from prisons around the state to reduce overcrowding. "In order accommodate all the prisoners backlogged in the jails, Smith sent more to St. Clair County than that prison had been designed to house—even as the plans had been revised to contemplate two inmates to each cell."[30]

Smith, nonetheless, in 1984 "basked in the glow of his own success" and "insisted the Alabama prison system had now outstripped the federal courts' ability to foster improvements and could face the future on its own."[31]

Less than a year later, state officials were reminded of the ineffectiveness of their solution:

In April [1985], 200 inmates in the new prison in St. Clair County stormed a guard room, occupied several administrative offices, and took the warden, his deputy, and as many as 30 employees hostage for a period of 11 hours. By early reports, the inmates were armed primarily with clubs and knives, but some witnesses said that two pistols and a shotgun were also used. Two hostages were beaten into unconsciousness, one female officer was raped, and three other employees were injured less seriously.[32]

Problems continued to plague St. Clair and the other newly built prisons over the decades. The doors haven't even locked properly in St. Clair for much of its existence.[33] In 2015, there was another riot, which in 2016 led to "several hundred inmates [being] transferred to other prisons, resulting in a population at capacity rather than far above it."[34] However, by the end of 2017, the population was overcapacity again, as it remains to this day.[35] Rodent and bug infestations persist, as outlined in this book, as well as violence, widespread health problems, and many other issues.

The accounts in this book show that sentencing policies, overcrowding, and other, sometimes seemingly smaller but related aspects of how the system is designed (how much toilet paper is distributed, for example) are more likely to blame for the buildings' crumbling infrastructure than either their age or the lack of additional prisons.

# Chapter 6

## "You Never Have a Moment's Peace"

WHEN I INTERVIEW HIM again in December, Tim discusses more problems with living conditions in the prisons, his experience trying to write a book while in prison, trying to get sleep, the causes of mental health problems in prison, and other topics.

Tim says the plumbing problems in the prison are "nasty," and that there are further issues with flooding in the prison when it rains.

"Sometimes when you flush the toilet, it'll come back up out of the floor drain," he says. Echoing what others have told me previously, he explains how when it rains, the water "comes in through underneath the doors, your exit doors in the dorms. When it rains real good, it pushes that underneath the door."

Tim also confirms that people are "throwing their blankets on the floor, pushing the water back toward the door."

* * *

In the last several months, Tim started writing a book about his life and the prisons he has been held in. I ask him what it's like trying to write a book while imprisoned in Bullock.

"It's hard," he says. "You normally have to wait until late at night, until everybody is asleep. Otherwise, there is no peace. It's hard to concentrate when there's, all the time, hollering, laughing, commotion going on. You have to wait until it's late at night. And then you have to get through the mental part of focusing on what you want to write about and not on the day surrounding you."

He is about five chapters into the project—"and they're not real long chapters," he notes. "But when I get toward the end of the book is when it's going to be a lot more detailed ... But it's hard writing a book, man. I just kind of started at one point, and I just kept going with it."

Tim enjoys reading as well. He is a big *Game of Thrones* fan, but he's read "lots and lots of books," he says.

When Tim first got to prison, he spent five years in lockup, the segregation unit, "because of my charges," he explains. "I had two cap cases ... and because of my charges, I couldn't go into population, so they had me in a segregation unit."

For "a very long time, I was back there in 23-hour-a-day lock-down," he says. "I'd come out of my cell one hour a day for phone use or shower. I stayed back there for 1,861 days ... And I done a lot of reading back there, because we really didn't have any TV, and all there was to do is sit in your cell and read. I read probably a couple hundred books when I was back there ... anything I could set my hands on to read."

Being in lockup for so long was "hell," he reflects. "It was truly hell. It was one-man cells, and they would usually have two or three people in a one-man cell. When you wake up in the middle of the night and you've got to go to the bathroom, you're probably going to step on somebody getting into the toilet."

\* \* \*

In writing his book, he is "hoping the right person, or the right persons, read it and be like, 'Wow, we can help this guy,' because I don't have a bunch of money, and my family doesn't have a bunch of money. So, it's kind of putting it out there in the blind, hoping somebody will see it. Kind of like a message in a bottle, throw it out there."

He's been in almost 10 years, "and I have a lot longer to go," he says. "My release date is 2050, and I'm 49 years old. All I can say about it is, 'Wow.'"

\* \* \*

Much like writing, it's also difficult to find the time and space to sleep in prison. Tim sleeps "an hour here, an hour there. It's really hard to sleep with a bunch of noise going on. Plus the fact that they're open dorms. And I just never have been able to get comfortable and sleep knowing there are people walking around me."

He feels he gets sick more often due to the lack of sleep, and that the lack of sleep makes him "grouchy" and "fatigued most of the time." He believes the lack of sleep is "one of the main reasons I'm in the mental health [dorm]."

He elaborates, "Pretty much everybody in this dorm, they've got listed under a mental health 'C Code.'" There is one level higher, the "D Code," but prisoners cannot be put back in the "regular population" until they are an A or B, he explains.

"Honestly," he continues, "most of the people in here, I think, have mental health issues *due to* the prisons, due to the environment that we're in. I mean, anybody who could endure everything that goes on in an Alabama prison and not have a mental health issue, something is wrong with that person. I've been diagnosed with PTSD, paranoia, bipolar disorder, depression issues. But, it's like, 'I wonder why...' Anybody who goes through all this and does not wind up with mental health issues, they've got bigger problems than I will ever have."

I ask if he was told why he was classified as a "C Code." "They've never really told me," he answers. "You can see a counselor who talks to you for a few minutes, and they write down what they want, and that's what it is."

Asked which aspects of the prison system most lead to mental health problems, "The environment that you're placed in, the shit that we go through," he answers. "I believe that causes a lot of people to be classified with mental health problems. You never have a moment's peace. You're always on edge [about] whether or not you'll get robbed, somebody is going to jump on you, this or that. It's an open bay dorm. 'Open bay' means it's one big room with a whole bunch of bunk beds."

\* \* \*

"The roach problem here is so damn bad that if I was to lift my mat up, there will be roaches scattering," Tim tells me. "If I open my drawer, my box, roaches will scatter. Everybody's bed or living area is infested with roaches. Everybody in this dorm has a roach issue. I've tried everything to [get] rid of them: bleach, soap, water. They just have not done what they need to do to get rid of them."

He's also seen rats in the prison, "especially around the chow hall."

Working in the kitchen in an Alabama prison is "disgusting," he explains. "It makes you not even want to eat. Everything is nasty. Nothing is really sanitary. The floors are busted concrete. Everything stays wet. It's nasty. They don't have anybody to make sure everything is clean like it's supposed to be."

He worked in the kitchen in Kilby Prison when he was incarcerated there toward the beginning of his sentence, "five to nine hours a day," every day, a job he was assigned, never compensated for, and that he could be punished for refusing to do.

He also worked as a "floor man" in Kilby, waxing and stripping floors, and was compensated only a tiny amount for that job. "They used to work the shit out of me," he says. Most prisoners are not compensated at all.

"The biggest thing was, once a month or once every other month or so," he recalls, "they would have inspections come through, and they would put all us [prisoners] to work, come down and put us to work, 'Get everything clean because they're coming through for an inspection.'"

# Chapter 7

## "Somewhere They Shouldn't be Able to House Humans"

THE WEEKEND AFTER CHRISTMAS, just days after my interviews with Derek about the plumbing disasters that week, which he and Jordan tried to fix themselves, Jordan was stabbed by another prisoner. He and several other witnesses described the incident to me in interviews in the weeks after.

While accompanying another prisoner to the medical ward, Jordan encountered an officer and told the officer about prisoners who are constantly assaulting other prisoners in his dorm. The officer then "came right back down here and told these guys what I said," says Jordan, "and he should not have done that." Other prisoners who witnessed the event back up this account.

After the officer told the prisoners what Jordan had said, multiple witnesses say, another prisoner confronted Jordan and a yelling match began. The prisoner rushed toward Jordan and the fight became physical. Jordan didn't know that the man had an ice pick. The man stabbed Jordan in the back.

Jordan was taken to a free world hospital, released in the early evening of the same day, and was brought back to the same dorm in the same prison. He called me the next day. Jordan says he was told at the free world hospital that the ice pick had missed his lung by an inch. The next day, Jordan was written up with a disciplinary slip for fighting. The other prisoner was transferred.

This all capped off the Christmas week in which the backed up plumbing system created disastrously unsanitary living conditions, which multiple prisoners have described, with Jordan and Derek reaching their hands into the toilet with garbage bags over their arms, down the drain, trying to pull out toilet paper and shit to relieve the system. They spent hours upon hours trying to manage the sewage water coming up through the drains and into the dorms, using their blankets to mop up the floor in a kind of Sisyphean nightmare.

* * *

The first week of January 2025, I interview a prisoner in Bullock who I'll call "Seth." He discusses living conditions, health issues, and other aspects of Bullock and the Alabama prison system. He is also one of the prisoners who witnessed Jordan get stabbed.

Seth has been in prison in Alabama for over 15 years, this time around. He was also in prison for a few years in the 1990s. He's now serving a life sentence and had been in Bullock for just a couple of months at the time of our interview, transferred from a work camp after a disciplinary. He beat the disciplinary charge but still has to remain in Bullock for a few months before he can go back, he's been told. He is in his late 50s.

At the work camp he was in previously, his job was garbage picking. He was assigned that job, never paid for it, and could be punished for refusing to work.

Some of the biggest problems in Alabama prisons, Seth tells me, are overcrowding, extortion, racial tension, sexual assaults, and other forms of violence. Bullock in particular is "one of the worst places I've ever been, man, especially the dorm that I'm in." He adds that he's already been "cludged out" since arriving at Bullock. He was slapped by another prisoner, hit the man back, then was jumped on by multiple other prisoners, "took me off the bed, slammed me on the floor and stuff."

"I'm trying to do the best I can to keep from using a weapon and stabbing one of them up," he continues, "and not being able to go home to my mother, because I've been gone so long, but you can only bite your tongue for so long. Pressure bursts the pipe."

He adds, "We had a stabbing in here yesterday, man," referring to the stabbing of Jordan. "It's awful in here, man."

During his two sentences, Seth has done time in every men's prison in Alabama. Most of the times he's been transferred, he explains, are "because of being cludged out and jumped on, sexually assaulted. You name it, and it's been done to me ... I got stabbed up 30 times over at Kilby. They tried to force me to run the tattoo spot. I told them I wasn't going to run it. They said, 'You're either going to run it or get off the dorm.' I told them they need to go get them some help. They came back and stomped me out. About 30 minutes to an hour later, they dragged me out of the bed again, stabbed me up over 30 times ... So, it's a blessing I even got breath in my body to talk to you."

Following the attack in Kilby, Seth had to be airlifted to hospital. Seth also had his ribs broken and a nerve in his lower back damaged after being beaten in Ventress Prison, and his leg "twitches by itself at night, and it hurts real bad. There's nothing they can do about it." All of his top teeth have been pulled since he's been in prison. His bottom dentures were left behind by a guard when Seth was being transferred, and he says he has to wait five years to have them replaced. He also contracted hepatitis C while in prison.

* * *

Seth too is experiencing the plumbing issues wreaking havoc. The plumbing is "backing up," he says. "It smells like raw sewage in our dorm. We've got roaches crawling all around our beds, all on your body at night. I mean, it's bad. It's real bad. Doo-doo all around the shower area and stuff."

In Bullock, "Most of the guys here just stay stressed out. With all the stuff going on, you have to stay on needles and pins. You don't know what's going to happen to you."

The food is "real nasty" as well, and he claims to have once found a "salamander-type thing in my food," not to mention hair in his food many times. Confirming what others have told me, he adds, "You go in the chow hall and it smells like sewage in the chow hall. And it's cold in the chow hall. It seems like there'd be some heat in there when we go in to eat, this being an all-inside place, but there's not. And it's cold in here at night ... A lot of us have trouble sleeping ... But it's just a corrupt place, man. It's somewhere they shouldn't even be able to house humans."

Seth sees "a lot of different health issues in the prisons. Some of the guys are limping around. Some of them are in wheelchairs." Many prisoners are "walking around with both eyes black, face beat up and stuff." He knows a prisoner who lost his vision in one eye when it was beaten blind with a broken broomstick.

When Jordan was stabbed the weekend after Christmas, "it happened right by my bed," says Seth. "One of them swung and the other one stabbed him in his back."

Asked how it impacts him to see things of that nature happen in front of him, he answers, "It puts me in a state of shock, from all the stuff that I done been through. It puts me as a nervous wreck."

In addition to all the times he's been stabbed himself, he estimates he's witnessed "over 25" other stabbings firsthand while doing time in Alabama, "throughout all the prisons I've been to," he says.

"It's dangerous. I mean, this new generation, that's all they know is to stab. You don't see one-on-one fights where you've got just two men, just fighting each other, and the best man wins, knuckles to knuckles. There is none of that going on. Most of the time, it's either four or five on one, and sometimes more than that," and often weapons are involved, he adds.

# Chapter 8

## "You Don't Know When to Go to Sleep"

IN EARLY JANUARY, I interview a prisoner I'll call "Chris." Chris is in his 50s. He has been in prison in Alabama for over two decades, in Bullock for the last few years, and like many sources in this book, he has struggled with various health problems while imprisoned, has not received adequate medical care, and lives his life in pain.

Chris has hepatitis C, high blood pressure, heart problems, "and other medical conditions," he tells me in our first interview. He also says he suffered a broken back as a result of a confrontation with law enforcement at the end of his brief and only stint on parole some years back.

Along with many other prisoners, Chris has been a part of civil lawsuits against the ADOC in the past, relating to poor medical care. The problems continue in Bullock, and the violence, the unsanitary environment, the overcrowding, and generally hellish living conditions don't help.

"This prison is really dangerous," says Chris. "I've been jumped on. I've been stabbed. I've caught a couple of stabbing cases myself." He's been stabbed twice in Bullock, and had "all of my front teeth knocked out," he adds.

"It's way overcrowded," says Chris, and "the plumbing here,

we just have water backed up all in the dorm, sewage." The food is "cold and nasty."

His medical problems and the lack of help continue. "It's kind of hard to get them to deal with [medical issues]. Right now I've got kidney stones real bad. I'm pissing blood," he says.

I ask if he's been able to get help for that. "No," he answers, "I've put in a couple of sick calls and I still haven't seen them." He says it's been a couple of weeks now. And between the kidney stones and the titanium rods in his back, "My back is killing me," he says.

In addition to having himself been a victim of violence in prison, like most all prisoners, he's also a witness to violence on a regular basis. The violence is all around one, "every day," says Chris.

"It's traumatizing," he elaborates, "because you don't know when to go to sleep. I'm already diagnosed with paranoid schizophrenia and PTSD. When they put you in that dorm in there, you don't ever see the officers but once a day when they come around, change shifts and count."

Chris continues, "There's so much going on at night that you don't know whether to go to sleep or stay up or what."

Throughout his sentence, Chris has been transferred to almost every prison in the state. "Probably here" is the worst, though, he says.

"The officers, they just don't care. The administration is crooked just like the rest of them. They allow all the beatings and extortions and stuff like that to go on." And there are "a ton" of drugs in the prisons, which, like virtually all the other prisoners I've interviewed, Chris says are being brought in by Alabama Department of Corrections employees.

"The prison is so dangerous, man, that you've got people in the prison that are homeless. When I tell you 'homeless,' it's because they don't have the beds because they're not strong enough to keep their own bed."

\* \* \*

A prisoner in Bullock who I'll call "Ed" has also been incarcerated for over two decades, in Bullock the whole time, which is unusual for Alabama prisoners with long sentences.

Ed was the prisoner mentioned in a previous chapter, who was permanently blinded in one eye by another prisoner wielding a broomstick handle several years ago.

"I was sitting on my bed, and the officers hooked the inmate up to jump on me, to attack me," Ed explains, "because I wrote the Commission on them, about what was going on in here, and the officers retaliated by putting [another prisoner] up to attack me."

He continues, "They let him in the dorm on me, and it was supposed to have been a regular fist fight, but it turns out it wasn't what it was. He hit me with a broom handle, whooped my eye out."

Asked what he had written to the Commission about prior to that incident, he answers, "About the food, and everything going on in here, and the treatment of the mental illness people, the way they treat folks in the prison, everything. And officers retaliated about that. They retaliated by putting him up to jump on me. [The other prisoner] admitted to it. He told me the officers put him up to it."

Ed adds, "I've been living with one eye since then ... So, I filed a lawsuit, and they dismissed it, told me the officers ain't do no wrong." He says officers have since bragged in front of him about getting away with it.

The hardest things about living with one eye are "getting around in here," he says, and "mostly, just putting up with folks calling me 'blind' and everything like that. I be having a hard time with them, and I can only see them with one eye. It's some of everything. I can't describe it. Some of everything [is hard]. You know?"

Ed elaborates on the living conditions in Bullock. "Bad, bad, living bad, the food is bad, everything is bad in here," he says. "They hardly feed you. They don't treat you right ... Somebody done something to you and they put you right back in the same room where they're at. They don't separate you. They'll put you back in the same area where the incident happened."

Plus, "It's way overcrowded in here. Every day, there's a fight in here. There's a lot of corruption going on in Bullock County right now, lot of corruption, and it needs to be checked into."

Ed claims to be innocent of the crimes for which he is doing time, and says the hardest things about being in prison are "doing time for a crime I didn't commit," and that "my family is dead except for my auntie, my uncle, and my two cousins." Losing family members while in prison "made me mad," says Ed. "The most difficult thing I experienced in here is losing my family. That's the most difficult thing I experienced in here."

### ＊ ＊ ＊

A prisoner I'll call "Zach," in his 30s, has been in prison for around two years. He was in two other prisons before arriving at Bullock over a year ago. In early January, Zach reached out to do an interview for the first time.

He describes the living conditions in Bullock as "run down. There's rust on all the racks. All of my sheets and everything have rust all over them from making the bed and all that, on some of my clothes and everything. It just gets on everything. The tiling in the shower is all torn up, and there are holes, stagnant water and stuff in the showers. This place is old and run down, and it'll take a lot for them to actually get it running back up to standard."

(As previously noted, Bullock actually opened in just 1987.)

He continues, "There's no real safety or security here either. There's a cube or whatever, but there's a cube operator in there, not an officer. I've seen fights and stabbings and all kinds of stuff happen, and the cube operator stands there and watches it happen and nothing is ever done about it at all. So long as the person doesn't end up going to medical, if they convince the person to get in the shower and clean it up and bandage themselves in the dorm, then nobody does anything. There's no kind of first response stuff at all."

Zach adds, "Oh, another thing: I was thinking that the whole Alabama scandal—there's this whole fentanyl epidemic going on [in the prisons]—I think there should be a mandatory, like every six months, first aid class for the whole camp, how to do CPR, what to do, because beating on the window and hoping that officers show up, and hoping that officer has Narcan on them ... There needs to be more of community support [for one another]. First aid. Like, nobody in here knows first aid. For real, they should have first aid training, CPR training, stuff like that."

Zach got this idea after his best friend in prison died of a heart attack several months ago. They enjoyed playing chess together. Zach hasn't played chess since.

"He had a heart attack, but they thought he was passed out on drugs, which he wasn't. He was 10 feet away from a bench full of people watching TV and passed out on the floor, having a heart attack, and nobody knew anything. Nobody knew what to do. But, if I had been on the scene, I could have given him CPR and at least given him a chance."

Zach says health problems are constant in prison, and that right now "there is staph everywhere. Every dorm has got multiple cases of staph. I've gotten it twice myself, had to get it lanced out and patched and stuff. I don't know where it's coming from or what."

It doesn't help that the laundry situation in the prison is "mediocre, at best," says Zach. "You can send your clothes out to the laundry and they might not even come back. Right now I've got one pair of pants that I've got to wear all the time."

Zach reminds me that "Bullock is a mental health camp," and he is "in a mental health dorm of the mental health camp. So, there's a lot of people here who don't know how to take care of themselves, or don't care about themselves enough to take care of themselves. So, they're dirty. The phones, coughing and sneezing on their hands and using the phone, or getting in the ice chest or the microwave. If we had access to Lysol or bleach, or anything like that, hand sanitizer of any kind, that kind of stuff would help... I've always gotten confused as to why we can't have that."

For Zach, the hardest thing about being in prison is "having other people dictate how I do my time, what to do, when to do whatever. The state has determined that I need to be in here for punishment. The people in here shouldn't need to punish each other for anything. The punishment is being outside of society," he says.

"Some of the other inmates get big headed and sort of start this little hierarchy or whatever between each other. And when they start implementing rules and regulations of their own, they kind of become the police when the police aren't around. Sometimes it's for the better. Sometimes it's just inconvenient. And sometimes it's just outright against how I want to do my time," Zach explains.

To get through the day, "I have a lot of hobbies," Zach continues. "I draw. I do soap carving projects, read books, write music, poetry, all kinds of stuff. I keep myself busy all the time. I don't like to sit around and be idle. I make decks of cards and play cards with people. Hell, a couple of months ago, I made a little bowling set out of Styrofoam cups and a sock ball and we went bowling in prison."

He reflects, "That's just what I do, man. I have this little quote still in my wallet, says to 'live a life worth the calling you received.' And I believe that one of my callings is just making this place a little less shitty every day."

# Chapter 9

## "All We Can Do is Pray"

"I STARTED AT A max camp, West Jefferson. That's where I first started ... But Bullock is worser than that Level C prison to me, as far as the stabbings and stuff like that," says a prisoner I interview in Bullock for the first time in early January. I'll call him "Nick."

"And you're locked down all day. We can hardly get any yard time. We barely ever get any yard time. See, I come from a prison where everything is on the outside, and get to Bullock, and everything is on the inside. And I've been playing softball ever since I've been locked up. That's the only recreation I really got is softball."

Nick has been in prison in Alabama for roughly 15 years. Like most prisoners in Alabama, he's been transferred around to multiple prisons in the state while serving his single sentence. He did time in three other prisons in the state before Bullock.

"But I just don't like it here at this prison, for real," he continues. "It's like a whole different breed of guys. Everybody wants to stab one another and stuff like that. And borrowing money is about the worst thing you can do in here, and not have their money when you tell them you're going to have it for them, because they'll be wanting to stab and cut on you and all that old crazy stuff, man. Thank God I got family and they look after me."

Nick is in his 50s. Like many Alabama prisoners, he has health problems now that he didn't have before prison. And like many others, the main health problem he struggles with is diabetes, easy to get and difficult to manage in prison.

"I've been diagnosed with type 2 diabetes since I've been in here. And they're going to feed you a lot of beans, a lot of starchy foods. So, how can I get around that diabetes, being here in an Alabama state prison? To me, they promote diabetes, because they feed you all this starchy food, with noodles and bread and beans. They promote diabetes, if you ask me," he says.

Nick took medication for diabetes and high blood pressure for a year. "In this prison, they say I had high blood pressure, said my body makes too much sugar and all this," he says. After a year of taking the medications, "My A1C never did come down, and I called my momma and told my momma I'm going to quit taking this medicine because it ain't doing me no good. And, believe it or not, I quit taking that medicine. My brother passed away. I lost 60 pounds. My A1C went down. They took me off the blood pressure pills. I haven't had a headache in about six years."

As we are doing the interview, I hear multiple voices yelling in the background. Nick seems unfazed, so I ask him about the overcrowding.

"It's very overcrowded," he answers. "You can reach over out your bed and touch the next man in his bed, laying in your rack. The racks are just that close together."

He adds, "Every prison I've ever been to is overcrowded," adding that Bibb Prison was probably the worst.

In addition to his own health issues, he remarks upon those of other prisoners.

"A couple of guys done got their legs cut off ... and a lot of guys are using the bathroom on their self. They don't need to be in here, for real. They need to be in Hamilton A&I, where aged and infirm people are at ... But [Bullock] ain't qualified to help people like that. So, they are not getting the proper help they need."

Nick recalls witnessing a nurse saying of an inmate who was having problems with his feet, "I don't care about his feet, because he don't care about his feet." Nick feels nurses shouldn't talk that way about patients, and believes that the prisoner in question "is about to lose his feet, for real."

Later, we discuss what it's like trying to sleep in the prison. Nick usually sleeps okay, "But, a lot of times, if a lot of people done went to sleep during the day, it kind of be hard for me to go to sleep at night. That's why I try to stay up all day and sleep at night. A lot of guys in here, they walk all night. I guess they want to be up. Every night in here is a late night if you want it to be, but I ain't ever been into that late night stuff in prison. I always want to sleep. I like to get my rest, but you've got some guys who like to be up two, three, four days at a time, but I ain't ever been that type of dude."

He continues, "They'll get on that ice [drug], and they'll wig out and they'll hallucinate, and they'll think people are watching. Then they'll start wanting to stab a man because he's watching and all that. It's crazy in here, man."

I was unable to speak with any officers working in Bullock in the course of writing this book, but a former officer who had worked in several other prisons in the state described Bullock's reputation in the following way in a phone interview:

There were some guys in [the prisons] who were men- tally ill, but they didn't necessarily get sympathy. People would beat them up and extort them and rape them just like everybody else [...] And the only thing they have [for people with mental health issues in Alabama's prison system] is Bullock Prison. And nobody wants to go there, because there are so many stabbings and killings. You have criminally insane people there. A voice might tell them to kill you in your sleep, and they might act on it.

So, a lot of people with mental illness, they're afraid to go there. It's crazy. It's very violent there. And they don't want to be there with all the guys who are criminally insane, who might not even have a real reason to attack you. They might just attack you randomly. So, nobody really wants to go to Bullock, so they just deal with their mental health issues all over the state.[36]

Nick is one of several prisoners I interviewed who witnessed the stabbing of Jordan the weekend after Christmas. Jordan "was standing in front of his rack. There's a walkway right between his rack and the man's rack. And Jordan is just standing there talking to the dude. And from what I seen, the dude that he was arguing with ran up to him. And I think they locked up, but [Jordan] bent [forward] and the dude hit him in the back, in the left side."

Nick reflects, "Ain't no way I'd stick an old man like that. I wouldn't do that. If push came to shove, if I had to, I would, but just on my strength, I wouldn't stab anybody. I ain't ever have that type of heart. I've always been the type of person to live and let live."

This is by no means the first stabbing Nick has witnessed. He saw a man stabbed in the neck in Bibb Prison, in a dispute with another prisoner over an unpaid debt. That was one of the scariest things Nick had ever seen in prison. Twenty minutes or so after that incident in Bibb, Nick learned that the prisoner who had been stabbed was dead, "and come to find out the dude that died, I grew up with his daddy. I didn't even know that was his son at the time, man."

Nick recalls how he played softball with that prisoner's dad "from the time I was 12 until we were about 32 years old, and come to find out it was his son [who got stabbed]. His grand-momma died two days prior to him getting stabbed and dying. I felt so sorry for that family."

* * *

Also in early January, I interview another Bullock prisoner I'd not met before. I'll call him "Max."

"It's rough," he tells me at the beginning of our conversation. "This ain't a place anybody would ever want to be, my brother." He's been in prison in Alabama for around two decades.

"I was a little teenager when I got here," he explains. "I was 16 when I went in the back gate at Kilby. When I got off the gate here at Bullock Correctional, I was 17. I've lost my mom. Every adult figure I had left in my family, I've lost all of them."

Max became a father when he was a teenager, before going to prison. "The only ones left alive now in my family ... are the kids and grandkids," he says, adding, "But, you've got to make the best of it, my brother."

I ask how he does that. "Just pray about it," he answers. "That's all we can do is pray about it and maintain ourselves and stay out of the way."

He says the biggest problems in Bullock are "stabbings, stuff like that, different things. We're not getting the proper mental health and medical treatment we need. We have no mental health counselors whatsoever."

He continues, "We ain't even got heat, no heat or nothing. The sewage is backed up, the drains and everything. The dorms we live in smell just like sewage water. It's awful."

The plumbing has been a problem "the whole time I've been here, but it's really gotten worse over these last couple of years."

In addition to prayer, to pass the time and get through the day, "I lay back, read books, draw, and I ain't good at drawing whatsoever, but I do ... my best. I be trying to put my talent to the test."

Asked what he likes to read, he answers, "Religious material, stuff like that. Anything to do with religious material, religious novels, books where people be writing different stories about where they've been in prison, how they live their life in here and out there and stuff like that."

* * *

In early January, I interview Chris again. Not long before our conversation, there was an overdose death in another dorm, and a prisoner was stabbed in the neck while waiting in line in the chow hall. Both events were confirmed by other prisoners after I spoke with Chris.

"And it's cold as hell in here," Chris tells me. "We have no heat in here. I mean, I'm telling you, it's so cold in here right now, I've got blankets, jackets, everything wrapped around me, talking to you on the phone."

Chris tells me almost everyone in his family "that hasn't passed away" has been locked up in Alabama prisons. His son got out recently. His daughter is supposed to get out soon. "It's real hard right now. I won't lie," says Chris.

"My wife, she passed away," he continues. "We pulled her off life support the day after Mother's Day, and my youngest son, he got murdered down in Montgomery."

It's particularly hard, says Chris, because "the state don't supply any of your mail stamps or your hygiene stuff like deodorant or anything like that. So, I've been without for a while."

Chris struggles with depression, "and I've been locked up for a long time. It's kind of hard, but I can't do nothing but take it one day at a time."

Asked how he gets through the day, he answers, "Mostly, I try to sleep it away, especially when it's cold like this. I mean, I've been trying to get me a job back in the kitchen. I had to quit that the year before last because I had a hernia, and I had to get a hernia operation, but I'm trying to get a job back in the kitchen. That way, I can at least kind of eat."

Asked what the kitchen is like in Bullock, he elaborates, "I mean, they've got a lot of sewage problems here, water problems, and the back-up from the drain backs up in all the sinks, the showers, the dorms, and it's real bad. They have problems with it backing up in the kitchen too."

Chris also discusses the role of mental illness in the prison.

"This dorm that I'm in here is a mental health dorm," he says, "and Bullock is a mental health institution. And it's supposed to have people that work here that've been trained and know how to deal with mental illness inmates, supposed to have patience, but they don't."

Compounding the mental health issues in the prison, echoing what many other prisoners have told me by now, prisoners in Bullock get "hardly any" outside time on the yard, Chris says, "maybe once a week, if that, usually maybe twice a month at the most."

Access to "law material," meaning the prison library, is also limited, "because they're always so short staffed that the law library is never open. They don't have the officer security to transport inmates up and down the hallway, control movement."

Even church, "We might get once a week, if not once a month."

Prisoners in Bullock, consistent with Alabama prisons generally, get one roll of toilet paper per week, which will be a theme through the rest of this book, as I've discussed it with many prisoners and believe I've discovered how the insufficient amount of toilet paper relates to the severe and ongoing plumbing and sewage crisis in that prison.

"One roll every seven days, and that's not enough," says Chris. "It causes a lot of problems. People run out [of toilet paper], and they have to use the bathroom, tear their shirts up and things like that."

# Chapter 10
## "Dirty Water"

Despite certain "dorm reps" (unpaid prisoners who have leadership roles in the dorms) trying to prevent and discourage drug use in his dorm, the problem is still rampant, Zach tells me when I interview him in mid-January.

Many prisoners "are selling their trays and their apples and their oranges and peanut butter sandwiches, and everything they can get, their mats, their blankets, everything they can, for flakka, for the most part, or no show," and several other prison drugs, he says.

"Flakka" is described by the Drug Enforcement Administration as "a dangerous drug that is similar to the street drug commonly known as bath salts."[37] "No show" is described as "a suspected synthetic cannabinoid-laced drug product."[38] "Ice" is a form of crystal meth.

Zach struggles with addiction himself.

"On a simple tip, I smoke cigarettes. I've been smoking cigarettes for 20 something years. So, there's that, but I also have a pretty bad ice addiction," he tells me.

Asked what it's like struggling with addiction in the prison, "I mean, most of the time, it's pretty easy. [The drugs] are everywhere, and if they're not here, they're right next door, and if they're not right next door [in the next dorm], they'll come to you. I mean, it's everywhere. It's easier to get in here than on the streets. I don't have to go drive across town and ride dirty or anything. It's just right there," he explains.

Zach says Bullock introduced a Suboxone program after three prisoners, Clifton King, Dustin Ortega, and Christopher McGhee, all died in a single 10-day span in April 2024, with two more prisoners being found dead the week following.[39] I haven't been able to ascertain if the causes of any of these deaths were made public.

* * *

Addiction to hard drugs is new for Zach, who has only been in prison for a couple of years, though he has decades ahead of him. Before prison, in addition to cigarettes, "I smoked weed a lot on the streets, but I wouldn't really call it an addiction. It was kind of just a recreational thing. I didn't even get introduced really to ice until I was in the county [jail]. And then it was so readily available when I got into the system that it just became a normal thing for me," he says.

Zach elaborates on the role of cigarettes in the prison and its internal economy.

"We can order cigarettes on the store. They come in Tops, roll-your-own. They have a regular menthol and they also have Grizzly Wintergreen dip. Pretty much, an economy revolves around what a Top is worth, for CashApp or whatever. So, you can buy Tops on the store for $3.33, but if you want to buy it from [another prisoner], you're going to pay him $10.00. So, if I go buy five Tops,

I can spend five Tops as $50, and go buy ice or flakka or whatever," he explains.

He can also buy extra rolling papers on the store commissary and sell the cigarettes individually, two for a dollar. "So, I can pay $3.33 on the store and then turn around and make $30.00" off one pouch of Top, "selling them individually and two at a time."

Asked how much toilet paper prisoners get, Zach confirms what other prisoners in Bullock have told me: "Well, we used to get two rolls a week ... Then, about a year ago, they cut us down to one roll every week. Then here, recently, within the past month, they said they were going to do two one week, one the next week, two one week, one the next week, but they haven't. They did two one week in December and then it's been back to one a week ever since then."

Zach continues, "Like I said, these people that are selling their trays and everything, they sell their toilet paper too. So, they get one roll of toilet paper. They'll sell it for one cigarette a week, and I don't know how they're using the bathroom. I guess they're taking a shower right after."

Asked what kinds of problems the lack of toilet paper causes, Zach elaborates, "It can be an issue. Sometimes when I run out, I've had to cut up a T-shirt into little squares and go that route, or go to the bathroom and then immediately take a shower right after. It's generally a cleanliness issue. And then if some of these people aren't properly washing their hands or using soap or whatever, then they're spreading who knows what, who knows where. When it was two rolls a week, it was manageable, and now it's pretty stretched thin. Here, I usually end up buying an extra roll or two from these guys with a cigarette so that I can make it through the week, but I don't know what they're doing."

Prisoners also get just one mini bar of soap a week, so they frequently run out of that, too.

When I ask Zach if it's common for prisoners to use their shirts or other items to clean themselves up after going to the bathroom because they don't have enough toilet paper, he answers, "Within the past probably six weeks, maybe a little longer, our whole sewage system for [two of the dorms] is completely backed up. And the maintenance had to open the pipes up and pull the shirts, blankets, sheets, smoking pipes, all kinds of crap out the drain, because it was backed up. You would flush the toilet and the sewage would come up through the drain pipes in the general floor area by the sink and showers, and it was backing up and pushing into the common areas, dirty water."

I'm not an expert on plumbing, but perhaps if prisoners were provided a sufficient amount of toilet paper, there would be fewer plumbing disasters.

Finally, Zach too notes that periods outside in the yard have been "few and far between. We get a tiny amount if we go to the store, but you're only allowed to go if you're catching store, and if you're not catching store, you're stuck inside. So, yard call is almost kind of out of the question."

# Chapter 11

## "Rarely Ever Get to Go Outside"

THROUGHOUT MID TO LATE January, I continue interviewing prisoners in Bullock. Since I started several months earlier, they've noted more and more that they are getting less and less outside yard time. By now, at least in the dorms they are in, they are only allowed to go outside if they have money on the store commissary, and then only to walk to the store and back.

At this point, prisoners have also been telling me they are very cold. Almost every single one has mentioned how cold he is while we are doing the interviews, describing all the layers he's bundled up in to come to the phone. It's hard to be awake. It's hard to go to sleep. Temperatures have been unusually low for the region lately. There's even been snow. And the heat is not working properly.

I ask about these and many other issues in our interviews.

"My dorm, which is a mental health dorm, is not part of the special mental facility they have, but this is like the in between," says Zach. "You're almost in population, but you're really in a mental health dorm. So, they kind of are rowdy and stuff in here … So, our freedoms are even more limited. So, if they're doing yard call, they'll do two or three dorms at once, so everybody will get to go out onto the yard. But, as far as this mental health dorm specifically, we rarely, rarely ever get to go outside. Like I said, if you go to the store, you can go, but then not even really either. You just walk outside for a minute to get to the store."

He continues, "As far as normal yard call goes, I guess it's, like, seasonal also. It's really cold right now. Last fall, we actually did get irregular yard calls probably once a week, sometimes twice a week, but that only lasted like five weeks ... As for right now, this current season, they haven't done a yard call in weeks. I can't even remember the last time. It was probably August."

Inside the prison, "It's really cold. I'm wearing sweatpants, two pairs of socks, pants [over the sweatpants], shirt and sweater and a jacket, and I'm still cold," says Zach.

There is a wide range of mental health issues in Bullock. "There is all kinds of stuff. There's full on schizophrenia. There's dissociative identity disorder. I have bipolar with psychotic tendencies. There are all kinds of different mental health codes. Some of them are mental health code A, but there's mental health code B, C, and D [prisoners] all over the place. There are a few dudes in here that just talk to the air all day long," says Zach.

"But, then there are people like myself," he continues, "who are—you've heard the term—like a 'functioning alcoholic.' I'm kind of like a functioning mental health patient. As long as I'm on my meds and I'm keeping my sleep schedule and everything straight, I'm pretty functional. If my sleep gets out of whack or I get too stressed out or anything, then my grip on reality will slip and I will start going off the deep end, which I really don't want to explain..."

Zach had been in psychiatric facilities in the free world before prison, and even then, he felt that being around other people with mental health issues made his own issues worse. "Being incarcerated on top of that" in such hellish conditions of course exacerbates the problem.

"And the treatment here in the mental health dorm is so minimal," he adds. "I see a doctor on a teleconference like once every 60 days, 90 days, and we talk for 10, 15 minutes and then that's it. And then it's pill call every night or whatever." At the separate mental health facility at Bullock, Zach says there are more resources and activities, "But, for the main camp, there is like none of that really, which is kind of sad, because I would like to have more counseling and more therapy and stuff like that available."

Throughout January, I also interview prisoners about the prevalence of suicidality. Asked if he has observed that people struggle with feeling suicidal in prison, Zach answers, "Yeah, I've seen quite a few people either try to hang themselves or cut themselves, or overdose on fentanyl on purpose. I've seen that a handful of times within the past year, probably about 10 times. Some of them are the same person, multiple attempts. Some of them are successful and don't make it back. So, suicide is a big issue."

Zach hasn't lost any close friends to suicide yet, but was good friends with Clifton King, one of several prisoners in Bullock who died in a 10-day span last April. Zach believes the cause of death was a heart attack.

Losing a close friend was "pretty rough," says Zach. "I still think about him every once in a while. He was a really good chess partner of mine. I don't even hardly play chess anymore off the back of that. So, that was the first real body I had seen. And then everybody else was trying to pour ice water on him and slap him awake and all that stuff, and they were like, 'He's still breathing.' And I was the one who was like, 'He's dead, y'all.' I was the one that pronounced my friend dead in front of a bunch of people that didn't know what they were trying to do, which is why, last time [we talked], I had mentioned, if there was a statewide first aid class that was mandatory, something like that, that would help a lot.

"And there are a lot of older folks in here too, with actual mental health problems. I know of guys that's had [a bunch] of heart attacks. If someone fell out right next to me right now, I would have to bang on the window, get the attention of the cube operator, who is not even an officer. The cube operator would have to get the attention of an officer, and the officer would have to come down here, assess the situation, give permission to send that person up to medical. Medical is probably a 5 to 10 minute run if you're carrying a person on a wheelchair or something, if the doctor is here, [which they are] probably not. There are just too many steps to get help, any kind of medical help. And that's just if someone falls out. If somebody is stabbed up or anything like that, they're bleeding out ... It's just really not safe."

* * *

"It's good to hear from you, Matthew. It's just been so cold in here, man," Nick tells me at the top of our next interview, before I can ask him any questions. "Man, I'm talking about: It's super cold in here. It don't make no sense for them to have us locked up in here and we have to be cold like this. You feel me? You've got some guys ain't got blankets. Some guys ain't got mats. Man, they've got to sleep on their steel beds. I know they're cold, man."

He tells me there was an overdose death in the prison recently as well. Other prisoners have told me the same. Overdose deaths are a regular occurrence in the prison, he says, mainly from fentanyl. "If it wasn't in here, they wouldn't be dying, and I don't understand how the government lets these people get away with it."

Nick discusses the ADOC's man-made toilet paper shortage and plumbing disasters. It seems likely that the plumbing disasters are in part caused by the fact that prisoners are given just one roll of toilet paper a week, frequently run out, and use other items to clean themselves. At the very least, it's not helping.

"We get one roll a week, and a lot of guys sell theirs at the time they get it. Then they get to flushing blankets and shirts and towels and socks. We stay with the plumbing right here, trying to unstop the drains around here. Then you want cigarettes so bad, man. You know you've got to go to the bathroom every day, but you'll sell your toilet paper for one cigarette, and it's gone in two minutes. I don't understand that, but you've got to understand: We're in a mental health dorm. So, people with mental health problems are going to do things that normal people ain't going to do. I ain't going to sell my mat. I ain't going to sell my shoes. I ain't going to sell my deodorant. I ain't going to sell anything I need."

Nick continues, "A lot of times, people that take care of their tissue, we try to make it last all week, but when you run out, you can't get no more from the administration. We get toilet paper once a week, every Friday morning. Every now and then, they give us two rolls, but mostly, it's one roll of tissue since I've been in prison."

I ask if he ever runs out himself. "A lot of times I run out," he answers, "but I get with somebody I know that will have some tissue, and I borrow a little bit to go use the bathroom. But, yeah, in here, all of us run out of tissue, because one roll of tissue ain't enough to last seven days."

Nick says he's almost always been able to find someone who will loan him some toilet paper when he runs out, because "I try to get along with everybody. I'm a people person."

It's extra difficult for prisoners if they have stomach issues or get sick. "There are some people with runny noses. I have known some people that just use their whole roll of tissue blowing their nose, and they can't get anymore," he says.

"Yeah, Alabama is a sorry piece of crap, for real," he reflects after a pause. "They've got too many of us locked up to be able to take care [of] all of us the way they're supposed to."

Echoing what Zach and multiple other prisoners in Bullock have told me about the lack of yard time, Nick estimates that after being in Bullock for longer than a year, he's been given yard time seven times, and he too says prisoners are allowed to go outside only to go to the store, meaning only if they have money.

"I'm fitting to show you some discrimination that they've got going on here, too," he says.

In every other dorm within Bullock, "When they call store, everybody in the dorm can go to the gym, if you want to." He was moved to several dorms where the same thing was true. But, now, "Since I've been over here in [this] dorm," he says, "you can go to the gym only if you've got money on your account. That's discrimination all day long. And everybody can see it ... And I'm just in here for beds' sakes. My mental health code is an A. People with B, C, and D, they got their mental health codes, but my mental health code is an A."

Compounding the problem, Nick feels that prisoners with mental health issues are not treated properly, and notes that, while many are on medications for their mental health issues, they are also surrounded by illicit drugs that prisoners and free world experts widely agree are being brought in by Alabama Department of Corrections employees.[40] "I know one thing: [Illicit] drugs and mental health medicine do not work [together]," Nick says.

In addition to rolls of toilet paper, he's also seen prisoners "in the chow hall give up their whole tray for a cigarette," he says, and they don't get much food to begin with.

"They feed us like third graders, man. About two or three hours later, we're hungry again," he adds.

Nick elaborates on the role of addiction to cigarettes and other drugs in the prison: "A lot of times, man, you can get a pack of cigarettes and you can get all the food you want, because a lot of these guys come in and they're going to sell their whole tray for a cigarette, or you can sell your chicken for a cigarette, or your fish for a cigarette, or your french fries for a cigarette. I just ain't ever been into selling my food. I'm trying to eat all mine."

Nick smokes "about four or five cigarettes a day," he says, and struggled with addiction to other drugs in the past.

"The same day I found out my brother passed, I started smoking flakka, but I eventually gave that up, ain't nothing but a waste of money," he says.

Asked what it was like trying to quit flakka in prison, he answers, "Believe it or not, I had an out of body experience one Sunday morning that scared me so bad that that just shut it down right there, made me quit smoking it, for real. You ever heard of people 'wigging out'? Yeah, I wigged out one Sunday morning."

He says the people who have it worse, when it comes to dealing with withdrawal and trying to quit, are the prisoners addicted to fentanyl.

"See, if they can't get it, their body hurts," he explains. "I feel so sorry for these guys, man. They be moaning and can't get it. Their body is hurting. Their nose is running. Man, it's real bad. And a lot of times, when they get it, they don't get it to get high off of it. They get it to make their body feel better. It's like a medicine to them."

# Chapter 12

## "Looked Down on as Lesser People"

"I DID WANT TO mention something," Zach tells me at the top of another interview, in late January. "I'm a part of the, I guess, gay community in here. So, it puts me in a group, I guess, of real mean treatment in here."

He elaborates, "At first, it was by choice. I was spending time with mostly good people. And in the past, I've had situations where I've been claimed—'You're mine now, do as I say or else' type situations—and that's even been here [in Bullock]. I'm just minding my own business, doing my own thing, and some big bully type guy will come around and start putting down on you, and taking your store, and possibly feeding you drugs and keeping you strung out so that you become dependent."

He adds, "I've been fortunate enough to be with a couple of good folks, but I've been in some other situations, too, where I've been raped and stuff like that."

Describing one of the previous situations in which he was claimed and raped, "Another prisoner was putting down on me pretty hard or whatever, and I tried to get away," Zach recalls. "I went to the police and moved to a different dorm. Well, he showed up [in that dorm] and started threatening me with knives and to keep robbing me, and he had some other friends in that dorm who pulled a knife on me. And then this other guy was like, 'I will help you if you do this.' So, I ended up getting in a situation where I was looking for help, but he didn't have a dog in the fight, this other guy, so he made me do some things I didn't want to do in order to try and get out of that situation." In other words, in exchange for protection from the first person who was going to rape and abuse him.

The abuse from that prisoner "thankfully only lasted two weeks, maybe a week and a half," says Zach.

He got out of that situation only after "a homeboy I did some time with in county jail," who was then placed in Bullock around the time this was happening, "found out I was in that situation and found another gay guy to hook me up with, and he was more of one of the nice guys, I guess, so we connected right away."

The friend from county jail also "helped me pay to get out of my situation and helped take care of me for a while," he adds.

Prior to this friend facilitating this new arrangement, Zach experienced oral and anal rape multiple times, as well as other physical and emotional abuse, he tells me.

In general, in addition to the physical and sexual abuse gay people are subjected to in an Alabama prison, "They're just looked down on as lesser people," says Zach, reiterating much of what Derek said in Chapter 1. For example, he elaborates, "You're not allowed to go in the ice chest. You don't know if you'll get to use the microwave. You can't touch anything that they touch."

He explains that in prisons where the showers aren't sectioned off, "You have to face the wall. You can't turn around and look at anybody, because they might assume that you as a gay person are looking at them in a sexual manner, and they're not gay, so they'll get upset and then it could become a violent situation just because you accidentally turned around in the shower to rinse your hair off or whatever. So, there's a lot of old prison laws and oppression in this world and in the gay community.

"It has its upsides too, when you connect with a like-minded individual, or someone that shows that they care, or pretends that they care, whatever the case may be," he continues. "So, it's got its upsides, but the general vibe is that, 'You're a fuck boy, punk ass...' It could be anything. It could be like, 'Your money is no good here.' If you try and sell some of your food off your tray or whatever, they don't want you touching the tray or anything like that, a bunch of little kind of BS stuff that adds up to add to the stress of the stressful environment."

Zach says he knows numerous prisoners in Bullock who have tried to submit Prison Rape Elimination Act (PREA) cases that were "completely just ignored."

As summarized by a 2020 NPR report,[41] "The DOJ has [...] found that Alabama was 'deliberately indifferent'[42] to pervasive prisoner-on-prisoner attacks and sexual abuse, and failed to maintain facilities that are 'sanitary, safe, or secure.'"

The report further quotes Governor Kay Ivey responding to the DOJ reports:

> Republican Governor Kay Ivey calls the report an 'expected follow-up' and says her administration will be 'carefully reviewing these serious allegations' and working with the federal government to resolve the issues.
>
> "I am as committed as ever to improving prison safety through necessary infrastructure investment, increased correctional staffing, comprehensive mental health services, and effective rehabilitation programs," Ivey says.

"We all desire an effective, Alabama solution to this Alabama problem."

That report is from 2020. As of this writing, Ivey is still governor. The violence has done nothing but worsen since.

# Chapter 13

## "The Worst Fear I Have is Dying in Here"

A PRISONER I'LL CALL "Nelson" tries not to keep count of the days, months, or years anymore, so he's "not 100 percent sure" how long he's been in, he tells me, but he knows it's over a decade and that he still has a few decades left. Instead, he keeps count of the amount of times he's been stabbed since he's been in prison, and there have been "over 42" of those.

Nelson has been transferred through many Alabama prisons throughout his single sentence and has been in Bullock for several months. I interview him for the first time in mid-January.

I ask what the biggest problems are in Alabama's prisons. "The lack of security," Nelson answers. "I've been stabbed over 42 times in prison, different events. And I'm not going to lie, I done stabbed over 25 people ... but in defense, and no times were the police present, period. And then you drop drugs in here, then people are not in their right state of mind. So, it's almost like adding fuel to the fire. We're already miserable because we're away from our loved ones. And then you throw us in here, then you throw drugs in here, then you throw weapons in here. I mean, what do you expect to happen? It doesn't end there."

Nelson continues, "I've been stabbed all in my face. I have multiple stab wounds in my face. We could count them, each one.

I have plenty. It's not ending, man. The worst fear I have is dying in here and not making it out to my folks."

His sentence is well over 50 years, but he hopes to someday get out earlier on parole.

Echoing what others have said about the lack of security in the dorms, particularly in cases of violent incidents and other medical emergencies, Nelson explains that in the dorm he's in now, "There's a fence, then there's another door. That separates us from the cube, which is a glassed in room from the cube operator, and the cube operator has to call an officer who is up the hallway and get somebody to run down here and come to one door then another grill gate to get to me and save my life. Now, that's not likely to happen. There are no police here [in the dorm], period, whatsoever."

Asked about the impact on his physical and mental health of being stabbed so many times, "It leaves you with PTSD," he tells me. "You get really paranoid of everyone around you, because everybody has a weapon, and [they have weapons] for the lack of security. I mean, I understand why [prisoners] have [weapons], because you have to protect your own life. But, like I said, when you throw drugs in here, it no longer becomes a situation of protecting your own life. Now it's that you're not in the right state of mind and you're trying to hurt somebody, maybe because, in your mind, that PTSD sets in and you imagine somebody is trying to hurt you, and it's not even there. That's what we're going through now."

Nelson has many physical health issues, largely as a result of the stabbings.

"I have many" physical health issues, he says. "I'm asthmatic, very asthmatic, and I have issues with my lungs. They are very weak. Due to stab wounds and due to injuries, I have a lot of nerve damage. I'm very sickly, so I can't really defend myself as much as I used to, but I put on a good front, because you have to ward off predators."

He adds, "It's serious in here, man. I promise you. It's dangerous. I haven't been here that long at this camp, but I've already been stabbed twice in here."

One of those incidents occurred when a prisoner who lived in a different dorm came into Nelson's dorm. "No police stops him, no police tells him anything, he walks right in like he's the tough guy, and he sees me, and remembers me from another camp, from another incident, and I guess he sees me before I see him and he hits me right in the face with a prison-made knife."

Previous stabbings have also occurred when prisoners have gotten in fights near Nelson's bed and he's intervened to try to "protect my space," he says.

There is constant tinder for arguments, fights, and stabbings to erupt.

For example, he says, "A couple times when I came into a camp, they assigned me to a [bed] rack. I come in. I try to get my rack, and somebody else is already on it, and he don't want to give it up, but I'm telling him, 'I was assigned to this rack.' They assign these racks and they send us in here, and the police don't come in here to make us get the rack, or make them give us the rack. No, they throw us in here, then we have to fight for the rack. We have to fight for a rack I don't even want to be on. I don't want to be in this prison, period. So, why do I want to lose my life over a rack I don't even want to be on?"

The overcrowding in Bullock and throughout Alabama's prisons in "ridiculous," says Nelson, confirming what every other

Alabama prisoner I've interviewed in over 10 years of doing this work has told me.

"You have a lot of people sleeping on the floor," he elaborates. "They have people sleeping in the grill gates in other dorms. This dorm is a little bit more organized: They've got people on the floor but not in the grill gate. That's a gate that separates [the dorm] from the door."

Furthermore, Nelson "was told that if you were a certain mental health code, you couldn't be around other inmates," he says. "So, that's what I don't even understand," he adds, as prisoners of all different mental health classifications are mixed up together in the prison.

Maybe it's the overcrowding, I suggest. "Exactly," he replies.

Similar to other prisoners I interview in January, Nelson mentions that it's "freezing in here."

Alabama saw snow and unusually low temperatures throughout January, the heat in Bullock is not working and the administration refuses to fix it despite widespread pleas from the prisoners.

Reiterating what others have said, Nelson says the administration "claims the heaters broke or whatever, but I haven't seen anybody come work on it, and I've been here for a little while."

He hasn't received any yard time of late either. Prisoners have reported not getting regular yard time, or any yard time for some, since going back well before the cold weather set in.

"I haven't seen it if they do [give yard time], so it has to be rare ... Like I said, I don't keep track of the days anymore, but I know I haven't been here long, and I don't see the outside at all. I haven't been outside at all," says Nelson.

* * *

"I won't lie and say I didn't partake in some of the wrongdoings in here," says Nelson in our second interview, later in January. "Like, I've purchased phones in prison, cell phones, but even then, the police, from time to time, they'll come in and do a random shakedown, which is where they go through all of your things to make sure everything is how it's supposed to be. And they'll take the phone, because I'm not supposed to have it, because it's prison contraband, but then turn around and sell it back to me. So, I've had the same cell phone two or three times."

Nelson was only recently transferred to Bullock and has not tried purchasing a cell phone there. "I haven't been here long at all. I don't know how this camp works. I won't buy something like that at a camp where I'm not sure, because a lot of people, they get stabbed and killed over those types of things, from other inmates trying to take it from them because they can't afford them," he says. "So, I normally wait a little while to see how the camp is running before I purchase something so expensive, because a phone here sometimes costs like a thousand dollars ... And I don't have money like that to just be throwing away."

* * *

Nelson says the only addictions he's struggled with in prison have been to coffee and cigarettes, but he quit drinking coffee. Echoing what others have said about the role of cigarettes in the prison, "It's crazy. You would think cigarettes were a drug," he says, adding that cigarettes are another thing "that a lot of people get hurt over, owing out cigarettes, packs of cigarettes."

Like many prisoners throughout this book, Nelson discusses the plumbing disasters and toilet paper shortage.

"Since I've been here, I've seen a lot of [plumbing issues]. They have a lot of issues with that. And I ain't been here that long, like I said. It's always flooding up and then it comes out in the drains and it smells like a sewer all through here all day, feces. You can smell it all day. I don't think that's healthy," says Nelson.

Reiterating what others have said, "You get one roll [of toilet paper] to make it through the week," he says, which causes all kinds of problems, some of which are likely related to the catastrophic plumbing system.

"You end up tearing your shirts, which could be a charge if they ever catch you," Nelson elaborates. "You tear up a shirt, that's destruction of state property. But what other choice do you have if you have to go to the bathroom?"

He's run out of toilet paper "a thousand times" himself, he says. "I've had to tear my sheet up. If they catch me, they catch me, but if I've got to use the bathroom, I've got to use it."

\* \* \*

Later, I ask Nelson about suicide in prison. Often, prisoners "are using a drug" to kill themselves, he says. "It's called fentanyl. It's some new age stuff. I don't know too much about the fentanyl. I just know it's one of the things they use."

Asked if he's around a lot of people who feel suicidal, "Thousands," he answers. "There's a lot of them. They feel like it at least once or twice a day. And they cut their wrists all the time, go to suicide [watch]. The police hold them in there for a couple of days and then throw them out. And I've seen a few times where they cut their wrists and the officers say, 'Go further. Kill yourself.' So, it's crazy. I mean, how much they care about a life in here, it's slim to none."

Nelson has done time in at least seven of Alabama's prisons during his single sentence over the last decade. It's common for Alabama prisoners to be transferred many times throughout their single sentence, often at random. Asked which prison was the worst of the ones he's been to, he says it's too close to call between five of those seven. In Ventress Prison in Clayton, Alabama, "I got stabbed in my sleep there. So, that's why I really didn't like Ventress."

✳ ✳ ✳

Throughout the state's prisons, "Like I said, there's no protection whatsoever, lack of security," Nelson says.

Using Bullock as an example, he explains, "They have the gate, then you have the doors, then you have the hallway. The health-care [unit] is all the way at the end of the hallway. So, even if they do make it in here to help you, you have to go far away to get help … It's too much. And they ain't in a rush."

Not only is violence rampant and medical care inadequate, Nelson notes that the public health risks associated with Alabama's prisons, in no small part caused by the extreme overcrowding, are serious. He points out that during the Covid pandemic and in the event of any similar event in the future, "If you needed six feet apart from each other, there's no way we would be able to do that. There's literally no way." (The Alabama Department of Corrections told me the same thing when I was working on my book *Doing Time*, written during the pandemic.)

Nelson's point here is an important one. Due to the unsanitary, overcrowded environment, the spread of illness is more likely. In an event like a pandemic, even if the prisons are in lockdown, employees will come and go and return to their communities, which aren't always in the same towns in which they work. Prison systems like Alabama's throughout the country can pose major health risks to everyone, prisoners and free world people alike, regardless of whether one feels that the inhumane treatment of the prisoners themselves is a justified means of punishment for a wide range of crimes.[43]

Take the issue of HIV/AIDS, for example, highlighted in Chapter 1. The epidemiologist Earnest Drucker, in his book *Plague of Prisons* on prison epidemiology, a book I highly recommend, notes:

The care of HIV-infected inmates is a major issue (and expense) in the prisons of states with high rates of AIDS. Thus New York State [...] has about 1,700 HIV-infected inmates receiving medical care using antiretroviral drugs, at an annual cost of more than $25 million. But best estimates are that these 1,700 are only about one-third of New York State prisoners infected (there is no routine testing of inmates). These HIV-positive individuals have a great need for testing programs to identify them and to initiate their treatment as early as possible—both for their own benefit and for reducing transmission risk in the prison and, on reentry, in their communities.[44]

He writes that "the association of incarceration and the AIDS epidemic is [...] very strong," and that "between 17 and 25 percent of all people in the United States who are estimated to be infected with HIV disease will pass through a correctional facility each year, roughly 190,000 to 250,000 of the country's estimated total of 1 million HIV-positive individuals."[45]

Furthermore, Drucker continues,

Recent evidence also suggests that cyclical patterns of release and incarceration may foster instability in sexual and social networks involving drug use, leading to broader social disorganization that increases AIDS transmission risk. In conjunction with unstable housing, untreated drug addiction, and recurrent imprisonment, a "churn" in social networks occurs that is now typical of these communities. These destabilizing effects act within the social networks established in the prison feeder communities of many cities to produce increases in risk for HIV transmission both by sex and by drug use. Two-thirds of prisoners return to incarceration within three years of release and subsequently reenter their home communities a few years later. This pattern of serial disruption spreads risk across these communities, affecting even those not directly linked to ex-prisoners. "Risk networks" can include drug use and sexual partners of ex-prisoners, who may form a bridge between this population's periodic exposure to the criminal justice system and the surrounding population.[46]

Alabama's prisons are known for outbreaks of tuberculosis,[47] scabies,[48] HIV rates that triple the rest of the state's population,[49] high rates of hepatitis C (about 17% of the prisoner population versus about 1% of the general population),[50] and plenty more. Some Alabama prisons were still reeling from a TB outbreak when the Covid pandemic began to hit the United States. According to the Marshall Project, in this context, in 2020, Alabama prisons saw a 47% rise in their death rate.[51]

During the worst of the pandemic, Nelson was in lockup in another prison. "A guy stabbed me. I stabbed him back," he explains, so he was experiencing a different hell than prisoners in general population for between 10 and 12 months of that time. He shared the lockup cell with another prisoner.

In lockup, Nelson explains, "They give you one shower a week, which I think is horrible. The trays are brought to you roach-infested. The light fixture is hanging out the thing, and that's how you light your cigarettes, the light fixture, which is dangerous. The wires are just hanging out openly, and that was really dangerous, because if you don't know what you're doing, you can easily shock yourself. No light in the cell. No bigger than a closet. You have the two toilets and the bunk bed. That's all you've got in the room. No light. Hot water don't work."

Throughout the prisons, he adds, whether you're in general population or lockup, "The living conditions are horrible. That goes without saying."

# Chapter 14

## "Happens All the Time in Here"

"It's been about the same old, same old" since our previous interview, "prison being prison," Seth tells me at the beginning of another conversation in late January. "Violence going on, folks getting stabbed, slapped around, beat up, folks getting high, folks extorting folks, all kinds of different stuff going on in this prison."

Previous chapters focused more on the stabbings Seth experienced and witnessed. In this follow-up conversation, I ask if he can elaborate on the sexual assault he mentioned in a previous interview.

About a year and a half ago, "Somebody gave me something, and I passed out and woke up that way," he says. He doesn't know who it was or what the person gave him, but he passed out, doesn't remember anything, and woke up to discover he'd been raped in his sleep. He got medical attention and stayed in Bullock's mental health dorm for a brief period.

Nobody was disciplined as a result of the incident. Seth assumes the person who did it "is still in prison somewhere, unless he got out ... I don't even know who it was. That's the thing. I've got to walk around and don't know. I could be living in the dorm with him right now, the same one that did it. I don't know," he explains.

"It's crazy," Seth continues. "It's like, a lot of the time, the ADOC, they don't bother to get your enemies. Then you end up in the same blocks with them and everything else."

Sexual assault "happens all the time in here," he notes.

## Chapter 15: Drugs, Bugs, Hernias, Violence, and "Corruption Officers"

"It's really bad in here. This place is flooded with drugs, man, and a lot of young people in here, they're overdosing. They ain't making it back home to their families," says a prisoner, who I will call "Oliver," when I interview him for the first time in January.

"You've got the police in here. They're bringing that shit in here, man," he says. "They make a lot of money off that stuff. Lately, they've been catching them. They've been kind of busting them a little bit, but you've got a lot of officers in here that are supposed to be corrections officers, but they're more like corruption officers, to me."

He adds, "And then all the stuff that goes on in the prison really falls back on them, because you've got to realize we're locked up. We can't go anywhere and get anything, so everything that comes in got to be brought in from somebody on the outside. That's how a lot of this stuff gets in, through the officers and stuff like that."

As noted previously, prisoners and experts agree that most of the drugs are being brought in by ADOC employees. Even when the prisons were on lockdown and closed to visitation during the pandemic in 2020, for example, drug-related deaths continued.[52]

The longstanding drug problem in the state's prisons has continued to get worse. As Eddie Burkhalter at Alabama Appleseed points out,

> Overdose deaths, and especially those known or suspected of being caused by fentanyl, have soared in the state's prisons. The overdose mortality rate in Alabama's prisons last year of 435 per 100,000 people was 20 times the national rate across state prisons.[53]

"You ought to see the stuff prisoners are doing just to get it," Oliver says, "just to get high. They're doing anything and everything. They're robbing people. They're beating people up, robbing them, taking their store bags."

Oliver has been in prison for almost two decades. Like most prisoners I've interviewed in Alabama, he's been transferred around to several prisons in the state while serving his single sentence. He is in his 50s.

"I've lost half of my family since I've been in here, but thank God I'm still making it," he says.

He's been in Bullock for the last few years, "And guess what, Mr. Matthew. It's not just here. It's everywhere. All over the system, it's bad."

Some other major problems he has witnessed are "police brutality, police jumping on people, putting them in the hospital," and, "It don't look to me that they're running the cameras back to really see what really happens."

Violence among prisoners is also a major issue, which Oliver believes is at least in part caused by overcrowding. "A whole lot of violence," he says, "people getting stabbed. And people might get—how would you say it—poisoned with fentanyl. If you want to kill somebody, that's the way to get away with it now. They just put it in your drink or your coffee or whatever. They put so much in there, and you drink it, and it kills you, and nobody knows what happened. Nobody knows where they got it from. So, therefore, it's a lot of murders going on like that too. That's how they've been doing it, or even someone rolls it in a cigarette and they go somewhere and smoke it and it kills them."

Later, Oliver discusses the problems with the infrastructure of the prison itself, including the plumbing disasters, which unpaid prisoners were trying to fix themselves by reaching into the toilet drains with garbage bags over their arms in an effort to unclog the system, and by mopping up sewage water in the dorm with their blankets. This was at a time when Alabama was facing unusually cold temperatures for the region and the heat in the prison was not working.[54]

"Let me tell you something," says Oliver. "About a week, two weeks ago, listen, we had so much water in the dorm, I swear to God we mopped up water for three days. You hear me? And then when you mop it up, the water is still backing up through the drain."

Weeks later, "We've still got that same bad smell in here, kind of like a septic tank, something like that. It's terrible, man. I guess they called somebody out here. So, I guess somebody did something to kind of, like, drain it a little bit, but we've still got a bad, bad odor in here, a real bad odor."

The prison is also "infested with roaches," he says, confirming what others tell me. "Even in the bed you're laying on, it's full of roaches. Roaches, rats, all kinds of stuff. I've never been in a prison with so many roaches [as Bullock]. I mean, they're in bed with you. They're not just crawling on the wall. They'll be in bed with you where you're laying at. But I don't ever see anybody come around spraying for the inmates or nothing like that. They don't have a bug man that come around and spray. I don't ever see anybody spraying for bugs or anything like that."

Oliver also discusses the physical and mental health issues that he and others struggle with in the prison. Asked if he himself has any physical or mental health issues that he did not have before prison, "Yes," he answers. "I really do have depression problems that are pretty bad, and I'm on depression medicine. It's probably because of the food that we have. You wouldn't believe this. Some of the food that we have, on the box is, 'NOT FIT FOR HUMAN CONSUMPTION.' ... That's the kind of food they feed you. God knows what it is. I don't know."

Many sources in addition to Oliver, including sources in Bullock and other prisons in the state, have told me they've seen that label on boxes of food in prison kitchens.

Oliver continues, "And a lot of people are having hernia problems. A lot of people in the prison are having to go out to the free world now to have surgery done for hernias, whatever you want to call it, and I don't know where that's coming from."

I've heard this from other prisoners as well and have interviewed a couple who have hernias. Beth Shelburne wrote a great piece in October of 2024 about a prisoner being denied surgery for his multiple hernias.[55]

"And we don't get any yard time in here," says Oliver, confirming what other prisoners in Bullock have told me about the lack of yard time, going back well before the cold weather set in during January. "They just keep us held down ... You're supposed to get an hour a day, every day, if it's not raining outside. We get none of that."

Asked how the lack of yard time impacts prisoners, "That brings on a whole bunch of other violence too," he answers. "When you keep a lot of people just cooped up together, so none of them is getting air or anything like that, just keeping them locked in the dorm together, man, that creates a lot of violence for some people ... Just being locked down, all day, every day. They're up all night. They're doing drugs, fights, stabbings. They don't allow us to get yard time at all."

# Chapter 16

## "They'll Embarrass You"

IN LATE JANUARY, I continue interviewing Nick. Though it's warmed up to 45 degrees outside by Nick's estimate, Alabama is still in the midst of a cold spell and the heating system in Bullock is still not working properly.

"The last couple of nights, it's been real cold in here, man. You've got to sleep with your jacket on," says Nick. "Or put your jacket on top of your blanket, got a hat on, two pair of pants. It's too cold in here for them to have us housed in here like that. And the food ain't no better. They feed us like third graders."

Nick is expecting the temperature to drop again, along with rain, in the days coming. When it rains, the generally poor prison infrastructure and the problems with the sewage system in particular combine to cause flooding throughout the building.

"Right now, it smells like a cesspool in here, for real. And we even had the sewage back up about three weeks ago," says Nick, referring to the plumbing catastrophes through Christmas and New Year's, and confirming what Oliver said in the previous chapter. That still, three weeks later, "Every time we go out the dorm to go to the chow hall and come back, man, we can smell it ... We can still smell it. By us being in here all day, we get used to that smell, but once we go out the dorm and come back, man, it smells just like a cesspool."

He continues, "Then you've got the officers coming in here to do the count, and they're telling people they stink, and, 'You need to bathe,' and all that type of stuff. Even when we're going through the chow line, you've got officers telling them, 'Y'all stink. Y'all need to bathe,' and all that old type of stuff. It's no way to talk to anybody, but they don't care. They'll embarrass you. They don't care."

Making matters extra cruel, the administration of course does not help prisoners maintain their hygiene or live in even remotely sanitary conditions.

"One roll of tissue a week, one bar of soap, and by the time you shower two times, two or three times, that bar of soap is gone," he says.

In addition to the insufficient amount of toilet paper and other hygiene products that all prisoners deal with, you've also "got guys that don't like to take showers," says Nick. "They've got mental health issues, I guess ... They kind of look over a lot of them."

One recent change to the prison, Nick explains, is that prisoners used to be allowed to bring a bowl to the chow hall during meal time and bring their food back to eat in the dorm, and that's not allowed anymore.

"Now they don't want us to bring bowls to the chow hall, and you can't take food out the chow hall. They're taking people's bowls. They're throwing them away," Nick explains. "They've been doing this about three weeks now. If you get caught with a bowl, they'll take your bowl and throw it in the trash can. It's crazy, man."

Asked if prisoners were given a reason for the rule change, Nick answers, "No, they didn't give no reason why. They just said they don't want any more bowls in the chow hall. For about the last three weeks, every day, Monday through Friday, they've been shaking us down coming out the chow hall. You've got three or four officers out there every day, and they're patting everybody down coming out the chow hall, trying to get their food, or seeing if they've got any food where they can throw it away. And a lot of guys be telling them officers, if they'd be more concerned about the prison than the food, they'd be better off. 'Don't be worried about the food, man. The state, they've got to feed us. They're barely feeding us anyway.'"

He adds, "I always try to keep me a little something in my box, so I can eat. And I'm a type 2 diabetic, so sometimes I feel bad and sometimes I feel pretty good."

# Chapter 17

## "Very, Very, Very Dangerous"

AT THE TOP OF an interview in late January, Nelson tells me it's been more of the "same old" since our last conversation.

"Lack of security, the lack of help, to help someone who is in need of help. They're understaffed. They don't even have enough officers to man each dorm. So, that's a safety, security hazard," he elaborates.

According to data from 2022, Alabama has the second most understaffed prison system in the country.[56] As of this writing, Bullock has 1,538 prisoners, according to the ADOC's most recent monthly statistical report, although it is designed for only 919.[57] The number of guards in that prison is not readily available, but prisoners say there are not many. Alabama's prison system consistently operates at between 160 and 170 percent of capacity,[58] "with some facilities operating at 272% capacity," according to a 2021 report.[59] As Prison Policy Initiative notes, "Alabama has an incarceration rate of 898 per 100,000 people (including prisons, jails, immigration detention, and juvenile justice facilities), meaning that it locks up a higher percentage of its people than any independent democratic country on earth."[60]

"It's unsanitary" in the prison, Nelson continues. "There's mold around the showers. It's really nasty in here. We smell sewage all day. I don't know if that's healthy, but I don't think so."

Nelson has been in prison for over 10 years, and there's a mold problem "at every prison" in which he's done time. "It's all over the ceilings. The camp I just came from, which was William E. Donaldson, when it rains, it's almost like the hallways go under water. They have to put boxes all over the floor just so you could walk through and not slip and fall," he says.

In the Alabama prison system, when it rains, it floods.

And when it rains in Bullock, "It rains over my [bed] rack. It comes from the ceiling."

Nelson also feels prison is not safe for people with disabilities and other vulnerabilities. "We have guys in wheelchairs," he says. "I mean, I feel like if they're weak enough to be in a wheelchair, then they shouldn't be in population. They should be somewhere they could be helped more, but they're in regular population with us. They're getting extorted, getting robbed, all types of stuff. That's not really cool, and nobody is going to help them, because then the problem is theirs, and nobody wants the problem to be theirs. Nobody really wants to die in here."

✳ ✳ ✳

Later, Nelson discusses the problem of suicidality in prison. Just a couple of days before this interview, a prisoner tried to hang himself in Nelson's dorm.

"I had to hit the window and get the police, because he was trying to hang himself. And I'm hitting the window and it still took the police a few minutes to get in here, and the other inmates had to grab him by his legs and lift him up," says Nelson.

"I mean, this is a stressful environment," he adds. "Some people can't take the stress that this environment causes. I can't tell you I've been to prison before, so I don't know what prison would be like. This is my first time ever coming to prison, but I've been gone over a decade. So, I could tell you this right here: If this is what prison is like, this is very, very, very dangerous. Unsanitary, unsafe, unhealthy, understaffed, overpopulated, those are the words I would use."

Furthermore, "The police brutality—I thought this was a hands-off camp," says Nelson. "You're not supposed to put your hands on people, but they do. That guy who tried to hang himself, they jumped on him, slapped him around, called him stupid, all kinds of stuff. It's not really safe. And they're really not there to help you. Half the time, the guys I know that have yelled out suicidal thoughts, the officers say, 'Do it.' They're supposed to send you to, like, a crisis cell when you say you're going to kill yourself, but they don't. They say, 'Do it. We don't care if you do it.' They're trying to provoke you to do it. That's how so many guys have so many cuts and stuff, because they have to go to the extreme to get the help they need. They've got to cut on their self, hang their self, just for the officer to help. But [the man who attempted suicide days before] gave the heads up. He said, 'Look, man, I'm feeling suicidal.' They don't care nothing about that. 'Oh, you're feeling suicidal? Then do it. Kill yourself.'"

Nelson has also known prisoners who "intentionally killed themselves with a drug," the drug being fentanyl. These suicide attempts were successful, he says. Often when people attempt suicide in other ways, "The other inmates, they will grab him and stop him. For instance, the other day when that guy tried to hang himself: he was hanging, but the other inmates grabbed his legs and pulled him up," says Nelson. "They lifted him up, and other inmates cut the rope with a prison-made knife. The officers came in and jumped on him. They came in, slapped him around, punched him in the back of his head, threw him on the ground, put him in cuffs."

In Nelson's view, one factor contributing to prisoners feeling suicidal in Bullock is "the lockdowns. We don't get any outside time," he says. And prisoners "have literally no help. And people, when you feel helpless, worthless, only a strong man can deal with that."

To get through the day himself, "I draw portraits," says Nelson. "I can draw really good. I can draw the whole dorm to a T, how it looks. I can draw a person. And the people, I can draw really good. But I haven't had the feel for drawing since I've been [in Bullock], because they don't let you go outside, don't let you do anything. There's no activities that I see that they allow here, and it's always on lockdown. If you're not going to church, you're not going anywhere. And then half the time, they cancel the church because they don't have heat in the church. The heater is broken, but it's been broken since I've been here."

He's been in Bullock for several months, but "I'm not 100 percent sure how long," he clarifies, reiterating what he's told me in the past, "because, like I said, I don't keep track of the days or the months or the years, but I know I've been in here quite some time, and I haven't seen the heater on. We've been walking around in jackets."

Asked if it's still cold, "Yeah, it is," he answers. "It's freezing right now. My hands are really cold, and I've got on a jacket with a sweater on."

# Chapter 18

## "Always Around"

SEVERAL OF MY SOURCES have struggled with addiction to hard drugs while in prison. Some have quit. Some haven't. Some hadn't done hard drugs before their time in Alabama prisons. Some had.

As a sidenote, it's illuminating to have interviewed prisoners here and there who were convicted of nonviolent drug crimes but committed violent crimes while in prison, and to have also interviewed people who were convicted of violent crimes who didn't start using hard drugs until they got to prison. They are examples of the system's failure at every level, for every kind of prisoner.

"The overdose mortality rate in Alabama's prisons [in 2023] of 435 per 100,000 people was 20 times the national rate across state prisons," writes Burkhalter.[61]

Struggling with addiction and recovery is a big part of life for many prisoners.

"I mean, coffee, cigarettes," says Nelson. "I mean, when I first came to prison, I won't lie and say I didn't [use drugs]. They had this stuff called 'no show' I used to smoke a lot. I don't know if they still sell it, but I struggled with it really hard. Trying to quit, man, was the worst, because it was always around. It was always there. So, it was a little hard trying to quit. But, me, I had support from my family. And my grandmother had passed away, so I was really tough on myself. So, I quit through them, for them."

# Chapter 19: Dorm Reps

IN THE LATE 1970s and early 1980s, as mentioned previously, Judge Frank Johnson found conditions in Alabama's prison system to be unconstitutional. Johnson laid out his orders to address the problems in the *Pugh v. Locke* case in 1976.

In this chapter, I'll just briefly focus on one of the orders Judge Johnson gave under the category "Protection From Violence," specifically, order number six in that category: "At no time shall prisoners be used to guard other prisoners, nor shall prisoners be placed in positions of authority over other inmates."[62]

Throughout these interviews, prisoners have used the phrase "dorm reps" many times, referring to prisoners who hold that title in Bullock. I was always struck by that, given the legal history and that it would seem to push the line of "having inmates in roles of authority over other inmates."

After hearing this phrase from a few different sources, I searched for articles and official documents outlining what a "dorm rep" is in Alabama prisons. I didn't find a lot, so I asked a prisoner in Bullock to elaborate. This was in an interview conducted in February.

"Normally, a dorm rep is just someone that is a mediator between the dorm and the police, maybe to have an inspection, or pass news along," says Zach. "They have meetings periodically, I guess."

Asked if they're assigned that job, he explains that the position is "assigned, or voted, or passed down, however it works out … The dorm rep that we have in here is one of those tries-to-run-everything types. Some other dorms I've been in, you wouldn't even know who the dorm rep was, but when a new guy comes in, they'll help him find a rack, stuff like that."

In other interviews, prisoners have told me that dorm reps are the ones trying to stop the drug use in the dorms, rather than the guards. Another prisoner recently told me one of the dorm reps, in an attempt to try to prevent people from sleeping on the floor, is threatening to beat people who sell their mats to other prisoners.

One article with information about dorm reps in Alabama prisons is by Kim Kelly, in 2024 in *In These Times*.[63] Kelly writes of a wrongfully imprisoned person named Alimerio English working as a dorm rep in Ventress Prison in Clayton, Alabama. She describes English's job as a "dorm rep" as follows:

He is responsible for the safety and well-being of 190 incarcerated men, many of them elderly or medically vulnerable. He handles custodial duties and maintenance, screens dorm visitors and is also the first responder for drug and health emergencies. In his scant free time, he runs a therapy and counseling group for his fellow prisoners. He consistently works 12 to 15 hours a day and, for most of the week, he is the sole individual in charge of the dorm; a retired prison chaplain comes in to assist him a few times weekly, but otherwise English is not supervised by any corrections personnel.

# Chapter 20: The Cold

THROUGHOUT JANUARY AND FEBRUARY, the cold temperatures persist in Alabama, unusually low for the region. There has even been snowfall throughout the state. The heat in Bullock continues to not work properly. I continue interviewing prisoners throughout this time.

"We've been asking them to turn up the heat, but I don't even know if they can," says Zach.

Multiple shouting voices erupt behind him soon after we begin the interview. From what he can gather, it's a dispute over whether or not something should have been microwaved. Eventually, the conflict quiets down and no one is hurt.

The officers "came through to do the count," says Zach, returning to the subject of the cold, "and there were a bunch of us yelling, 'Hey, turn the heat up. Turn the heat up,' and they didn't really respond."

I'm surprised the officers aren't more bothered by the cold themselves, I reply.

"Yeah, well, they've got these big old windbreaker coats with fur around the collar," Zach explains.

It snowed the week of this interview. "Everybody is kind of on edge, fiending out for cigarettes and coffee, because the store was supposed to run Tuesday and they're talking about not running the store until Thursday because of the weather or whatever. It messes up the truck and stuff."

He estimates there are about four inches on the ground, and it's the "first time I've ever seen snow this far south. I'm from Huntsville, Alabama, and if it looks like it's about to snow, the schools shut down and everything."

Zach had previously been working on a soap carving project for a friend but hasn't been able to complete it due to the difficulty of focusing in the cold. "I haven't really gotten out of bed to do it, because I've been hiding under the covers for the past three or four days because of the cold. I'm starting to shiver right now," he says.

Asked if he knows when it's supposed to warm up, "I don't," he answers. "I honestly don't pay attention to the TV or the news or anything. That stuff kind of depresses me."

\* \* \*

"They used to usually give out extra blankets in real bad winters, when it's really cold," but they haven't done that this year in Bullock, at least not for cold weather, says Derek.

"They had gave us all the extra blankets already to soak up the water when the water was running really bad," he elaborates, referring to the chronic plumbing disasters. The "extra" blankets, to the extent there were any, were used for that.

Prisoners were "starting to talk about setting fires in here the other day," he says, and were "running around with torches and stuff, because it got so cold in here, but they remembered when [prisoners] done that before."

Derek continues, "And if they think it's smokey in here when we're smoking a cigarette, shit, well, set them damn blankets on fire and see how smokey it is. Everybody will be on the floor."

Derek is considering a different course of action: "I've thought about just writing a request to the warden about the heat," he says. "I'm going to maybe try to get everybody in here to write a request to that warden about the heat, try to get a goddamn pile of them on his desk by next week. I'm going to try to get everybody to write him a damn request. They'll have requests coming out of their ass." (Bullock has three wardens.)

He elaborates, "That's what [the officer] said. Everybody heard him ... When they came in to do the count, a couple of the fellas went over there, asking them, 'What about the heat? There's no heat in here. It's freezing in here.' 'Write a fucking request.' Come on, man."

He goes on: "It had to have been below freezing in here. It had to have been. And it ain't nothing but concrete and steel in here, so everything is cold."

Before the end of our call, I ask Derek if he believes the plumbing issue is related to the insufficient amount of toilet paper provided to the prisoners. Like the other prisoners I've asked, he believes it is.

"Sometimes these guys flush blankets and sheets down the toilet. If they don't have enough toilet paper to wipe their ass with, they're going to cut up stuff to wipe their butt. So, yes, that has made plumbing disasters in this place," says Derek.

$$* \ * \ *$$

"The last couple of days have been kind of rough, Mr. Matthew," says Oliver when I interview him again in late January. "We don't have any heat, man. It's bad. No heat. Air coming through the windows, the doors. We've been freezing."

I ask what kind of impact this has on him and other prisoners. "Ain't nothing we can do but just stay in bed, man, stay warm. It makes us not even want to get up and walk around," he says, adding, "The best thing we can do is just stay in bed, covered up, stay wrapped up."

On at least one night, "Officers had to spend the night in the prison. They couldn't even go home, it was so bad. It was so bad, they had to work a double shift until the snow melted, because the other people couldn't get here," says Oliver.

"I ain't ever been so cold in my life. I got worried the last couple of days. You could lay in your bed, Mr. Matthew, just be laying there, and you see steam come up out of your mouth, man. It's that cold."

* * *

In early February, Bullock warms up slightly, but the heat is still not working, and the temperature in the prison soon drops again. Furthermore, new issues make the prison even colder, exacerbating a variety of problems throughout the month.

In our next call, Derek updates me on his plan to try to get as many prisoners as possible to submit complaint forms about the heat not working.

Since then, "Yes, sir, we did that," says Derek. "We filled out the request slips and put them in the box for them to check on the heat. And I can't tell any difference, man. It's freezing in here to me."

Asked how many prisoners he estimates submitted complaints, "Oh lord, I can't say for sure about that," he answers. "We got a whole packet of request slips, which is about maybe 100 to a pack. So, we passed them out, but I can't say who filled them out and who didn't. I just went around asking them to do that, because that was the only way we were going to be able to get anything done."

* * *

I interview Derek again later that same week.

"Everything is just messed up in here, man. I'm telling you. Cruel and unusual punishment," he says at the top of the interview.

"Everybody in here is sick," he says, "especially the old men. They're all coughing and hacking and stuff. It's freezing in here." He estimates that about half of the people in his dorm of 80 or so are sick.

Derek and all the other prisoners I interview that week (more than are included in this chapter) report that, in addition to the heat not working in the prison, the hot water has stopped working as well.

"Our water is cold. Man, we can't take a hot shower," says Derek in late February. "I took a shower earlier. I was freezing to death. I've been cold for like three days, but I had to get in the shower earlier. There wasn't a choice about it. I had to do it."

That's not the only problem making the lack of heat worse since we last spoke.

"Prisons are made of concrete and steel," Derek elaborates. "You know that. Up top, they have a ceiling area through where all the electric wire and all that stuff is running through, but it has a breeze going through it. Well, the maintenance people came in here the other day and they took a bunch of lights down in our dorm. Anyway, when they took those lights down and took the wires and stuff out of them, they left the holes open. And these holes are just flooding air through them. It's like having a little air conditioner right here over your bed. We're all cold."

Furthermore, "They're starting fires in two dorms," says Derek, and, "They're talking about doing that in [this dorm]. See, that's what I'm telling you. The prisoners are fixing to buck. I know. I've been through this ... This is something that I've seen and witnessed with my own two eyes, being here and being amongst them. I've seen them buck, and they don't want that. A lot of innocent people, bystanders, are going to get hurt over that."

He continues, "If they decide to buck—and they say they are going to buck—if you don't ride with them, then they're going to consider you being police, and they're going to fuck you up. So, if they do buck, everybody has got to ride."

Prisoners in at least one other dorm have already started fires in the days leading up to this conversation, "especially since we've had this cold spell going through here ... They're getting ready to do it up here," he reiterates.

Asked what the prisoners who are contemplating making torches or setting fires are hoping to accomplish, "They're hoping to accomplish getting heat. It's so damn cold that they're setting fires to get heat," Derek answers.

As noted previously, one might think the guards would be

more bothered by the cold, thus providing some added incentive for the administration to get the heat fixed, but the ADOC resources issued to deal with the cold are of course more robust for guards than for prisoners.

The guards "got on these thick toboggan caps with fur on them and shit. They've got coats with fur collars and stuff like that," Derek explains.

At the risk of pointing out the obvious, it seems cruel to make people live in an environment in which employees have to be dressed for these cold temperatures in order to work.

"But this is the point I'm trying to get to," Derek continues. "They're fixing to start beating up the officers and taking their coats and shit from them. That's what I heard this morning. That's going to cause a lot of problems, a lot of friction."

* * *

"Man, the heater in here is not working, and it's cold in here. The water is cold. The heater ain't blowing hot air. It's just too much, man, and they don't want us to have any sheets up to try keep ourselves warm," says Nick when I interview him in late February.

Confirming what other sources have said, he says that "they took the old light fixtures down, and they have holes in the ceiling, and the cold air is coming through the ceiling. Even the heater vents are blowing cold air."

Nick also confirms the outbreak of illness in the prison that week. "There were so many people in here coughing and coughing and coughing last night, it was unreal," he says, "and the hot water boiler is still not working. The water has been cold for at least five or six days now, and it's too cold to get in a cold ass shower. And you've got to stay cold all day. We went to the chow hall last Sunday. Man, it was so cold in that chow hall, our hands and toes was numb when we got back in here. So, that can't be right, man. They've got us locked up, and we're living in this shit cold all the time, bathing in cold water. That ain't right, man."

Asked if there were fires being set, "Not that I know of right now, but we were talking about doing it this morning," Nick answers, "but our dorm rep told us that it ain't going to be a good thing to do." However, "I heard they did it over in [another dorm] a while back, and they had so much smoke in the dorm, it started making people cough and stuff, and they had to open all the windows and let the air out," he says.

"It's too cold in here," he adds. "I've been telling my family about it, man."

I ask if he feels there is any risk of a riot. "Eeehhh, there don't seem to be right now, but there probably will be if they don't get something fixed around here," Nick answers.

Asked how he gets through the days dealing with the cold, "Believe it or not," he says, "I take my coat, and I put it on top of my blanket at night, and I take a T-shirt, and I'll put it at the end of the bed and tuck it in to keep my feet warm. But, the blankets, man, the blankets are so thin, you can see through them. You can cover your head up with the blankets, and you can still see daylight. You know that if you can see daylight, air got to be coming through them."

He adds, "You got some guys in here that ain't even got any blankets. A lot of guys sell their blankets."

Nick also confirms what others have said about how the officers deal with the cold.

"Most of them got on their big old coat with fur around the neck of it, and they're dressed for the cold," he says, adding, "They can get extra clothes. We can't get extra clothes. Then they'll tell you to take your hat off. Man, we'll go walking down the hall, 30 degrees in the hallway, and they'll tell you to take your hat off, but they've got their hats on."

Asked why prisoners are not allowed to wear their hats in the cold, "I don't know what's the reason, but [the officers] always keep their hats on," he answers. "See, a lot of them wear skull caps and a lot of them wear baseball hats. They'll tell us to take our hats off, but they still got theirs on. Like we don't get cold."

Nick warns me that he's "about 15 feet from the main door" to his dorm, and that "when that door opens, I might have to get off the phone because there's too much air coming in."

After a pause, he adds, "Man, there's got to be something done about this Alabama prison system."

* * *

"Right now, we're freezing in here, man. We don't have any heat, hot water, nothing, man," says Oliver when I interview him again in late February. "I don't know what's going on with that. They said they're working on it right now. But, man, we've been freezing," he says.

"I hope I can get blessed one day and live how I want to live," he adds.

"Man, they've got holes," he continues. "They came in here and took some of the lights down [from the ceiling], and they left the holes, where they were running the wires through the holes, probably 12 or 13 holes that they left wide open. It's cold in here, man. It really is. It's so cold in here, man, you don't even want to go to the chow hall and eat."

I ask if he's heard of anybody starting fires in the prison. "I heard that some people in another dorm did," he answers, "because it's so cold. That's the only way they can stay warm. They've got to make a fire in their dorm. We haven't made one in here yet. We were talking about it, but we don't want to do something to bring problems to us. I don't want to do anything that's going to make me get in trouble and all that. But, one thing about it is, if the whole dorm stands up, then they can't write up everybody. So, we really were talking about it this morning, making us a fire in the dorm. Man, it's just that cold in here. So, hopefully they get working on it. Hopefully it'll get better, man. That's all I can say."

* * *

"I've been sick damn near two weeks. I've got a bad cold. I probably have pneumonia, man," says Jordan when I interview him again in late February. The heat and hot water have not been working, and many prisoners are sick.

"This place is so cold, man, ain't no heat down here in this building, man. And it's messed up. I've been sick, man. That's probably why I sound so funny today. They ain't got no heat down here in this damn prison, man, and no hot water. Nothing, man. It gets down to 19, 20 degrees, man," he says.

He's "been laying under the blanket for about two, three weeks," he says, adding, "Man, I'm thinking about building me a fire inside the prison camp. I know I might get wrote up, man.

Ever since I got stabbed, man, it's felt like everything has just been going downhill ever since then. Things have been bad in this prison. This is a messed up prison down here in Union Springs. And then when you go to the chow hall and sit down to eat your food, man, it's so cold in this prison, you can't even eat, man. It's probably 19 degrees in the kitchen, man. It's freezing around here in Bullock. I'm trembling talking to you, man. I've been in the cold all day, man. I went to the doctor. The doctor told me I might have a trace of pneumonia."

Jordan knows five or six other people with pneumonia in his dorm, he says.

Asked if he's submitted complaints about the heat, "Man, we told the warden. I told the head warden. I told the deputy warden. I told the damn lieutenant. I told the captain. I told the sergeant. I told the COs. I told everybody," he answers, adding that he and other prisoners even asked loved ones in the free world to call the prison to complain about the lack of heat.

Jordan tells me that once, years ago, when the heat broke down in Bullock, prisoners were temporarily transferred to a private prison in Perry County. Much like the plumbing issues and many other problems in Bullock and throughout Alabama's prisons, the problems with the heating system in Bullock are longstanding.

An article in *AL.com* in 2010 describes the incident that Jordan was referring to from that year:

> Alabama Department of Corrections spokesman Brian Corbett said 100 of the inmates were transferred to the Montgomery County Jail, and 450 to a private prison in Perry County. The move became necessary after two

boilers at the prison broke down over the weekend and a bitter cold wave swept into the state. The sister of one of the prison's inmates said [...] her brother had told the family that the facility had been lacking heat and hot water for a week, and that heat and hot water had been sporadic for about a month.[64]

A brief report in *The News Courier* out of Limestone County at the time laid out the financial implications:

It has cost the Alabama Department of Corrections $132,000 to house inmates elsewhere after boilers at their prison broke down during the state's cold snap.

About 650 inmates are back in the Bullock County Correctional Facility after a boiler breakdown and bitter cold forced the state to move them to two other locations.

*The Birmingham News* reports [...] that $108,000 was for housing 450 inmates for eight days in the Perry County Correctional Center.

The privately run prison in the Black Belt charged $30 per inmate per day. Two hundred Bullock prisoners were housed for eight days in the Montgomery County Jail at a total cost of $24,000, based on a daily charge of $15 per inmate.

There were more than 1,300 inmates at the prison when the boilers broke down, stopping most heat and water.[65]

Jordan was one of the prisoners transferred to Perry County Correctional in 2010. He tells me the ADOC never paid the private prison for housing the prisoners during that stretch, which is why they haven't sent them back when this has happened in the years since. Asked via email, the ADOC has declined to comment on whether that is true.

I ask Jordan if he believes there is currently any risk of riots in Bullock due to the poor living conditions, lack of heat and hot water, spread of illness and other issues, "There's a big risk, man. There's been the fires in [another] dorm. There's a big risk of riots around here. It might be any day, might break out today, man. They've been hyped around here, man, for the last two weeks, man," says Jordan.

"Them people got fires lit inside of their dorm, man. The drawer where you put your clothes and your stuff in the drawer, on your bunk, them tin, steel boxes, they're putting fires in there, man. They're setting fires so smokey that the dorm is about to smoke itself out of here," he says.

"So, people have already started fires?" I ask.

"Yeah, they're already doing it," says Jordan. "They've got to stay warm, man. They've got to stay warm somehow."

"In the dorm you're in?" I ask.

"No, down the hallway," he says. "They're talking about doing it in here though. They're talking about doing it today in here, but the other guys said, 'Man, don't do that. When they did that last time, they nearly killed themselves,' and they wasn't lying, man. Said, 'Please don't do that, man,' and because they'd open the doors [to get smoke out] and we like to keep to our own damn self."

He also adds that, "They don't even call no yard call for us," reiterating what other prisoners have been telling me over the months. "It's sad, man. This is a messed up prison. They need to shut this prison down and condemn the kitchen, man. When you go to the chow hall, it smells like a septic tank ... There's a septic tank right up under the kitchen. Man, it stinks so bad around here, and when you eat, when you go to the chow hall, you can taste that smell. That ain't right, man."

Previously, prisoners have described how guards are no longer letting them bring bowls of food back to their dorms from the chow hall. Jordan elaborates on that:

"People were taking their bowls to the chow hall and bringing their food back to the dorm, because it smelled so bad down here by that kitchen, but now they'll start crushing our bowls up ... Now we're taking our garbage bags and tearing the plastic, and putting it in the plastic, and try to stick it down by your privates and try and sneak it out the kitchen, but they're still catching us doing that, but we've got to do something to try to survive in here."

I believe Jordan has been in Bullock the second longest of any of my sources in that prison.

"Whatever them guys be telling you about this place is true, man," he says. "It's for real. Everything is for real, what they're telling you, man. It's a messed up place in Alabama. They told us a long time ago, 'Don't go to Alabama.' When they tell you, 'Don't go to Alabama,' don't come to Alabama. Don't go to Alabama prison. Please don't."

\* \* \*

In March, I reached out to the ADOC for comment on the problems with the heating system in Bullock Prison. The ADOC did not respond to multiple requests for comment on various aspects of this story.

Indeed, the ADOC has not responded to numerous requests for comment in the years since my book *Doing Time* was published. To be clear, I don't believe this is personal, or has anything to do with my work. It seems the two main sources who were in touch with me when I wrote that book no longer work there. And, of course, I assume the Department is quite busy. In any event, I'm just saying, it's been a while.

By early March, though the heating system is still not fixed, the weather has warmed up a bit outside and prisoners say the administration has at least tried to improve the hot water with modest results, but that after a few people shower consecutively (in a dorm of over 80 people) the water goes cold again.

January and February were brutal months in the prison. By the end of February, prisoners had reportedly started fires to keep warm. Others throughout the prison were considering doing so, discussing whether or not to start rioting, filling out complaint slips, appealing to all levels of employees from the officers to the warden.

It's worth bearing in mind as you read this chapter that the Department of Justice reported in its 2019 *Notice Regarding Investigation of Alabama's State Prisons for Men* that a "February 2017 inspection by engineering consultants hired by ADOC noted that not a single facility has a working fire alarm."[66]

Many prisoners have gotten sick. It seems the ADOC's strategy has been to ride out the unusually cold weather for the region rather than pay to fix the problem.

At the end of February, in the midst of all this, as the conditions grow increasingly inhumane and the prisoners increasingly agitated and unwell, as tension builds between them and the guards, I conduct a first interview with a Bullock prisoner who

I'll call "Cecile." Cecile has been in Alabama prisons for over 15 years, mostly in maximum security prisons, transferred throughout the state during her single sentence, as most Alabama prisoners are. She has been in Bullock less than a year.

Cecile spent a lot of time in Holman and participated in the riot there in 2016, in which fires were started and the warden and an officer were stabbed, probably the most significant Alabama prison riot in recent history that we know of. The events went on for a couple of days.

I interview Cecile about her previous experiences and her thoughts on what is happening now in Bullock. Cecile is a transgender woman.

Of the prisons in which she's been held, she spent the most time in Holman. "I've been to Holman five different times," she says. "Holman is wild. You remember back in 2016 when they had riots and they had all the stuff on the news about the cubes getting set on fire and the warden getting stabbed and all that, the police getting stabbed? Yeah, I was one of the ones involved in that."

She reflects, "It was crazy. They was oppressing us. They was coming in, putting their hands on us, taking our stuff, and just handling us wrong. They have the standard operating procedures they have to go by, too, and they wasn't going by it. So, we bucked on them, and it got a little wild, and the warden got stabbed. The police got stabbed. It was crazy."

According to the ADOC's spokesperson at the time, "About 100 inmates [were] involved in the riot."

I ask what that experience was like for her. "It was wild," she answers, "because I did two years in lockup, almost got a free world case behind it too, but they dropped the free world case and they just gave me a disciplinary and made me do two years in segregation. It was wild, because my family was looking at me like I didn't want to come home, like I didn't love them anymore, and all that type of stuff."

I ask her to elaborate on the motivations behind the riot and how prisoners organized to do it. "Well, we was in a dormitory setup where there's like 180 people to a dorm, and the dorms are separated between A, B, C, D, and E dorms. E is in a trailer outside the camp. And we all was getting on some shit where we were going to come together and stand up against our oppressors and not continue to let them handle us and put down on us.

"So, when the officers came into the dorm, they tried to spray us with the mace and all that," Cecile continues. "That's why they ended up getting stabbed. And the warden came in and tried to push one dude. That's how he ended up getting stabbed, because we all came together as one, and unified, and tried to fight against them and tried to make the situation and the conditions better for ourselves. And they did shut Holman down, kind of sort of, a couple of years later behind that. They've still got E dorm open … But they condemned … the main camp. They shut that down."

*The Montgomery Advertiser* reported on the announcement at the time:

> The Alabama Department of Corrections will close the main building and dormitory at Holman prison, relocating more than 600 prisoners to other facilities around the state in a move Commissioner Jeff Dunn called 'the culmination of years of neglect' of Alabama prison facilities.[67]

They of course kept the state's only death chamber running, however. As Dunn told *The Advertiser*, "[C]urrent plans are to maintain the execution facility[,] which will 'require basic utilities,' and the department is [...] in discussions with engineers and other experts about how to do that." Holman, too, has a notoriously problematic sewage system in one of its tunnels. Plumbing and sewage disasters are a recurrent theme throughout the system.[68]

Looking back now on her experience with the 2016 Holman riot, "I wish I could change it," says Cecile, "because it's really what's still keeping me in prison. What I done to come to prison is not what's keeping me in prison. So, it's kind of like I regret it, but it happened, so I can't take it back. So, it's something that I've got to live with. You know what I'm saying?"

Asked if the riot brought prisoners together in any way, "Yeah, it did. It brought people together, but it was more of a violent stand than anything, than a peaceful stand," she says.

Cecile says other longstanding problems with the prison system in general, which prisoners are dealing with now in Bullock, are "the food, and the temperatures in the dorms, as far as the heat and the air or whatever. The food is just horrible. You wouldn't feed a dog some of the stuff that we eat in here."

She reiterates something that many prisoners have told me over the years, that there are boxes of food in the kitchen with labels that say "NOT FIT FOR HUMAN CONSUMPTION." But, "They still feed it to us, though," she says.

"And the temperatures are kind of up and down, for real, because there's no heat really in the dorms. It's really just like living outside, for real," she continues. "That's why a lot of us are sick with runny noses, coughing, colds, chills, and fevers and all type of stuff. They really don't have enough medical assistance and stuff to tend to everybody's problems. So, they're really just overlooking it, for real, and it's contagious, so you will really get other people sick off you being sick. So, it's really starting to be an epidemic, for real."

She says illness is "going around in every dorm, for real. Every dorm in the camp, you've got people that are sick ... To go to the infirmary, or the healthcare [ward], to get medical assistance, they make you fill out a sick call slip, and it really takes two or three days before they even screen you for the sick call for your medical problem. So, it's not like you can go to the emergency room like on the street, like in the free world, in society."

Cecile might have come up for parole earlier, she tells me, but while in prison has gotten "violent disciplinaries like stabbing cases and some things that I'm really not proud of, because they're violent, but there are things that I was pushed, that I was coerced to do, because I have to stand my ground. I have to stand up for myself in here, because I really don't have nobody but myself in here. By me being transgender and by me being gay, it's like I'm outcasted. And nobody sticks up for me. Nobody stands up for me. Nobody speaks up for me. So, I have to do it for myself."

I ask if she'd ever done anything like that in the free world. "No, I'd never stabbed a person, never," she says, adding that Alabama prisons "will turn you violent, just because you have to stand up for yourself and stand your ground."

Focusing on Bullock specifically, Cecile feels "the staff members, they don't respect us. They don't respect us as much as they do at the maximum security prisons," she says. "The respect level is totally different. They talk to you crazy here. They put their hands on you. Officers jump on you. They smack you around. They spray you. They do all type of stuff."

Further, the overcrowding "causes a lot of stress and depression on us," says Cecile, "because it's an open bay dormitory, and it's not a cell block, so you really don't have privacy. Everything is out in the open."

Discussing the heating problems and the recent cold weather, "I went to the window and looked outside and seen all the snow on the ground," she says. "I haven't seen snow like that in my whole life other than when I had went up North, when I went up to Boston, Massachusetts one year when I was like 13."

Cecile tells me the heat is still not working "and they came in and took some lights out the ceiling, and the part where the lights go, there are holes in the ceiling, and there's air coming through the ceiling from where the lights are supposed to go. They took like 20 lights out the ceiling and there's air coming through the ceiling, and it's blowing right down on our bunks. There's no heat in the dorms. It feels like we're outside in the freezing cold."

She and other prisoners she knows have complained, "but there haven't been any changes."

* * *

From late February through early March, I continue interviewing prisoners about the cold, the heating and hot water systems not working, fires started, riots contemplated, and other topics.

I continue interviewing Cecile through late February and early March about the situation as it is evolving in Bullock.

Asked if, based on her experience, there's been any risk of a riot in the prison at any point in the past couple of months, she says it's been relatively quiet compared to her previous experiences in Holman, but that, "Just the other day, a white guy got into it with an officer in the chow hall, and they got to fighting and the dude took the police's night stick from him and beat him with it. That happened the other day, the other morning, in the chow hall with [an] officer."

Cecile continues, "The officers have just been over edge ever since, been putting their hands on people, jumping on folks, just out of retaliation over what happened to their co-worker. So, it's kind of crazy in here right now. They took our snack line from us today," she says, adding that, "Even though we didn't have anything to do with it, we're still being punished for it."

With the lockdown comes "controlled movement. They restrict your privileges like store privileges, snack line privileges, library privileges," and more, she explains, and some of these "privileges," like yard time, Bullock prisoners hardly ever get anyway.

Cecile confirms that there have been fires set in Bullock in recent weeks and months: "It was cold, and they had a bonfire going down there in [another] dorm. They were trying to stay warm down there. That [dorm] is at the bottom of the camp. They had some big fires," she says.

Although the temperatures have finally warmed up a bit (without the Alabama Department of Corrections fixing the heating system through the entirety of this winter) problems with the weather and the prison infrastructure continue year-round, and storms swept the country the weekend of our interview.

"It's been raining a lot lately, the last couple of days," says Cecile. "Water comes into the dorm when it floods. When it's raining outside, the water leaks into the dorm and it causes a big flood in the dorm by the doors, because if you don't put any blankets or anything down to stop that water from coming under the doors, it's just leaking right into the dorm. It's like that in every part [of the prison]. Even the gym is halfway flooded."

# Chapter 21: Convicted as an Adult While a Child, Growing up in Adult Male Prisons, Being Transgender in Prison

CECILE HAS BEEN IMPRISONED in adult male facilities since the age of 16, and remains so now. She was initially sentenced to 25 years to be served in adult male Alabama prisons, with the possibility of parole before turning 18. That was over 15 years ago. Her charges are for crimes in which nobody was physically hurt. She's been transferred through many of Alabama's prisons at this point.

In March, she discusses being transgender in prison, coming to prison as a child and growing up there, ideas for how to improve the system, and other topics.

Transgender prisoners are "outcast, and we don't get the same amount of respect that the men get, because we're considered 'sissies' or 'fags' or 'queers,' and it's like there's a different set of rules for us than there is for the men, for the guys," says Cecile.

"In the chow hall," she continues, "people look at us as, 'They're not supposed to eat behind us, drink behind us, smoke behind us, any of that stuff,' but on the street, in society, it's not like that. People drink behind women. They smoke behind women. They eat behind women. It's just, in here, we're looked at like we're creatures or we're disgusting or something like that."

Trans prisoners, like gay prisoners and prisoners diagnosed with HIV, are frequently harassed and assaulted, Cecile tells me. "We're picked on a lot more than the guys, because we're considered to be the weaker links," she explains.

Cecile has been physically assaulted many times in prison, including sexual assaults, and was sexually assaulted in recent years in Holman Prison.

There have been some positive aspects to life as well, however, loving relationships and friendships built.

"I'm in a relationship now with Seth. We're together. We take care of each other. We look out for each other. We're here for each other ... By being together like that, we watch each other's back. We feed each other. We provide for each other, and it's amazing ... I like it. I respect it. And it's a healthy experience for me, because I've had other guys in prison I've dealt with where it's been nothing like the relationship that I have now with him," she says.

✳ ✳ ✳

Asked what advice she would have for lawmakers, administrators, the public, anyone with a say in the prison system, about how to improve the living conditions, not just for gay and trans people but for anyone in prison, she answers, "I would try to aim at the death penalties and the life-without-paroles, because that's kind of like cruel and unusual punishment, because nothing is worth taking a person's life away from them, as far as being in prison for their whole lives, because everybody deserves a second chance. So, I would try to pinpoint that right there even though I'm not a lifer. I don't have life without [parole]. I'm not on death row. So, I can't say what their experience is like, but I know guys that are on death row and do have life without parole ... I feel for them, man, because I couldn't imagine spending the rest of my life in a place like this. I did half my life already. Half my life has been spent in here. So, it's just that I feel for people who've got to do the rest of their lives in here."

I ask what it was like being a child in adult male prisons in Alabama. "Wow, scary," she answers, "real scary. I actually came to prison when I was 17. I did most of the time [before that] when I was 16 in the county jail, but I came to prison when I was 17 and turned 18 in Kilby."

Kilby is the first prison that prisoners are sent to in Alabama. They can spend weeks, months, or longer there while it's decided which prison they'll go to next.

"It was just crazy, scary, wild," Cecile reflects. "You've got a lot of older guys that kind of cling to the younger guys, and they try to overwhelm them with some of the prison games and all that. It's just amazing. It's crazy, the things I've been through growing up in prison, and having to fend for myself."

Cecile was in the Bloods when she came to prison, she tells me, and "had a few people on my side that would stand up for me, or stick by me, and be there with me through the troubles, and good times and bad times."

Despite many scary experiences, "For the most part, the older guys try to guide the prisoners to positive trails, take programs, mind your own business, be respectful. There are prison codes inside of the prison that people live by, and I picked up a lot of them codes when I was real young. That's what's made it to where I've been able to survive this long since I've been in prison."

Human Rights Watch reported in 2017:

On any given day, approximately 50,000 children in the United States are held in correctional facilities. The number represents a 50 percent drop from 1999, but is still one of the highest rates of juvenile detention in the world. Every US state allows children to be tried as adults under some circumstances, and approximately 5,000 child offenders are held in adult jails or prisons at any point in time.[69]

# Chapter 22: Conclusion

I CONTINUE TO INTERVIEW Seth in late February and early March, while the heat is still not working and before the hot water was reportedly fixed in Bullock. To my knowledge, the heat was never fixed.

"Just dealing with this crazy old shit going on in here. You can hear how loud it is in here, lieutenants and guards and all them, they're coming in here and getting metal pipes from people and taking them to jail and all kinds of shit, man. They don't believe in writing disciplinaries or anything. You can get beat up in front of the police and they don't care. They'll send you up there to medical and patch you up and send you right back in the dorm," says Seth at the beginning of our conversation.

He continues, "Then they came in here and took the light fixtures down and left holes in the ceiling, and it's freezing cold in here, and our water in the showers is freezing cold, man. A bunch of us in here have been four or five days without showering, to keep from getting sick. We've put in sick calls to go to the dental, or put in sick calls to go because we've got runny noses and colds and stuff, and they haven't called us. Now, I put in a sick call a week ago and they haven't called me yet. Cecile put in a sick call to go to the dental about five days ago and they haven't called her yet. There's a bunch of us in here that's been putting in sick calls. They haven't called us."

Asked how many people in the dorm he would estimate are sick, he says that "out of about 80-something" in his dorm, "probably 40" are sick, "about half of us."

I ask if he and others filed complaints about the heat not working. "Yes, we filled out grievance forms and turned in grievance forms," Seth answers. "And hell, they won't answer them. It's like we're stuck in a box, man, being treated any kind of way, like we're not human. It's cruel and unusual punishment, what we're going through."

Seth is considering trying to encourage prisoners to come together and take legal action.

"We could file a 1983 Civil Act lawsuit on it, and that just takes forever and ever and ever. I'm going to contact my lawyer [who is] with DOJ. I'm going to let her know everything," says Seth.

He reiterates, "They came in here and took some lights down and there's holes in the ceiling where the air is coming all in the ceiling. They ain't got no plastic on the windows, none of that, man. They're supposed to pass out double blankets. They haven't passed out none of that stuff for us when it's cold in here like this. It's just cruel and unusual punishment going on."

Seth gives other examples of what he also feels are cruel and unusual punishments:

"The food. We go in there to eat the food, man. There's very little on the trays. I mean, a three year old, you'd feed a child more than what we're eating, man. They're starving us ... You might as well say that. Yeah, they're giving us enough to say they're feeding us, but that's it," he says.

"And the officers, they talk to us nasty and crazy. They threaten you [that] they're going to put their hands on you or something, cuss you like a dog, just cruel and unusual punishment," he adds.

I asked him to elaborate on what it's like dealing with hunger. "I'm hungry right now. On the days like today, there ain't but two meals, man. And I had a diabetic form that I brought with me from the other camp where you can go eat ... The diabetics eat three times. They have to feed the diabetics three times. Hell, I try to go out the door and they say they can't understand the writing on my papers, so they tear my paper up and tell me I've got to get a new paper, that I can't go eat chow. Come on, man," he says.

* * *

"There's a bunch of people in here sick," says Derek when I interview him in late February. "A lot of people sick in here, coughing and hacking, pooping on themselves, peeing on themselves, and they can't help it. Some of the old dudes that are doing that, I've been knowing them since I've been in here, almost 25 years. I know them. I didn't like them back when they were young, and I don't like them now that they're old, but it don't change the fact that they're still human beings and they ought to be treated as such."

At a couple points as we're talking, there's a little commotion in the background. The first time, Derek says a lieutenant just came into the dorm and he might have to get off the phone. He asks the officer, "We good?" He tells me the officer says we're good.

A couple minutes later, he interrupts himself again. "The warden just walked in, brother. It's Sunday. What the hell is she doing here? If she's here ... I don't know what's going on," he says.

He says he'll stay on the line unless they ask him to get off.

"I ain't going to get off. I'm just telling you now. She's standing here super close to me. I almost can't talk real loud," he says. Then I hear him put the phone aside and talk with someone. I can't fully hear what is said. There's yelling further in the background as well. Soon Derek comes back to the phone.

"She wanted to know if I was on the phone with somebody. I said, 'Yes, ma'am,'" he explains. "She's in free world clothes now. She used to be in a blue uniform. I've been knowing her for a long time. I've been knowing her ever since she was a sergeant, worked her way all the way up. She's all the way up to a warden now."

After he gets a little space, he continues, "It's getting worse down [where] they're starting fires and stuff like that, and a friend of mine—you know him, you've talked to him—told me this morning when he came in from working [in the kitchen] that they're fixing to shut the chow hall down and that they're going to have to bring food in trucks to people, because the floor drains in the kitchen are not working. There are only two drains in the kitchen that are working, so they're going to have to close the kitchen down, I reckon to do work in there, and do whatever, fix the drains, however long it's going to take them to do that. They're supposed to close the kitchen down."

* * *

Things have been "about the same" since we last spoke, says Seth when I interview him again in March. "You can't imagine the stuff going on in here. You can't daydream this, none of that shit. It's crazy, man...

"We're still waiting on them to come fix our heat. They said the boiler is out. There is no hot water. It's been cold. They're trying to get the boiler fixed, so they can fix our water. It's gotten a little bit warmer—the water has—but it's still not hot. I mean, it's warm, and after two or three people get in the shower, it's freezing cold again."

Thankfully, "It's warming up outside a little bit," he adds. "They've kind of got the windows open to get a little fresh air in here."

* * *

Seth discusses his relationship with Cecile and the importance of positive relationships in prison.

"She's my best friend," says Seth. "Me and her hang all day, every day together."

He notes that transgender people are often looked down upon, mistreated, and even feared in prison, "but [Cecile] is a good person, a real good person, got a good heart and ain't no troublemaker, for real. She's done been in some stuff since she's been in prison, but sometimes we get put in positions where we have to do things."

He reiterates, "Me and her, we're real close. We're real tight. We hang with each other every day, go to chow hall together every day. I mean, we do everything together, just about. She's my best friend ... You've got to have somebody you can trust and believe in, who is going to be there for you."

\* \* \*

Days later, we talk again. "Nothing has really happened. It's all about the same," says Seth. "We've got one dude who thinks he runs the fucking dorm."

"Is he the dorm rep?" I ask.

"Yeah. They won't do nothing with him, man. These people let him get away with anything. It don't matter. I done had my lawyer talk to COs about him slapping these guys in wheelchairs and different stuff, doing the shit he's doing and getting away with it. They've done nothing about it. Administration has done nothing with it. That just goes to show you, man, being here slapping folks around in wheelchairs, that shit ain't good."

\* \* \*

"A couple police got their head busted at this camp and another captain got stabbed at another camp, Ventress Prison," says Oliver when I interview him in March. "There's a lot of violence going on, for real. They kept us locked down for a little while, but they eventually let us off."

\* \* \*

I am not a prisoner, a lawyer, a criminologist, a public health expert, or much else. I have my informed opinions. I have my feelings. But I do not pretend to know the solutions to the problems with the prison system exposed in this book. Furthermore, many

Americans are okay with or supportive of the prisons we have in this country, even the worst prisons, and I don't judge anyone for holding that perspective, particularly when they've been victims of violent crimes. I'm not telling anyone what to think about all this. I consider my job in this book to be documenting the crisis, showing the readers what they are supporting, opposing, or not seeing.

That being said, prisoners have the most experience of anyone with the system. So, throughout March and April, I mix questions about potential solutions to the crisis into our interviews.

I ask Oliver what would make the prison system more humane in Alabama or in the country in general. "When [officers] get caught [breaking the law], they give them the option: 'We can prosecute you, or you can resign right now and you'll never hear nothing about this,'" he says, adding that they "usually resign." He says "a little thing they could do" to improve the system is, "if they get caught breaking the law, then they should be in prison like we should, just like us."

I ask what he feels could be done to solve the overcrowding problem. "I would say start letting guys' sentence be their go-home date. If they give you 15 years on a life sentence, once you do 15 years, you should be able to go home, not go up for parole and get turned down five years."

He adds, "That's who has got to decrease the overcrowding: the parole board. They're not letting anybody make parole. They're setting people off five years at a time. They set some people off five years that don't have five years left in prison. It's terrible here in Alabama ... That's the only thing that'll stop it: Let some people make parole, man."

(Sidenote: I've also interviewed prisoners who have been

granted parole and still have to wait in prison for a release date not knowing when it will come.)

I ask what he thinks of the Alabama government's longstanding and contemporary proposed solution of simply building more prisons. "They can't keep up maintenance on the old ones, so how are they going to keep up maintenance on the new ones?" says Oliver. "We've got no heat in here or anything."

Asked what he thinks of Governor Ivey in general, he answers, "I don't know what's up with her. I don't understand her, man. See, when she first got into office, she acted like she was down with the people in prison. And then when she got in, she made a 90 degree turn ... And I think she's too old to be Governor anyway. She's too old."

*  *  *

"They finally took us off controlled movement, and they got stuff moving back around, the store running and stuff," says Seth when I interview him again in March. I ask Seth too about solutions to the problems.

"For the DOJ to come in, take all the drugs out of the prison system. Just make it a whole lot better. Put more programs in there. And then when you've graduated from certain programs, make you eligible to go home. Different course programs. Say you've got 10 years to do. You've got a program that you can go to that's like two or three years long, and once you take it, it'll cut your time [before parole]. They could do all kinds of different stuff for us, but they don't make any programs. They make money off us. That's it," says Seth.

"Anger management courses," "coping courses," and "college courses" are among the ones he'd like to participate in, but even when programs are available, "We take them to help us go up for parole. We go up for parole and we get set off five years. I ain't going to come in here and do all this to get my education and get myself together if you ain't going to let me go, if you're going to deny me parole and set me off five years and hold me."

Furthermore, the prisons themselves "are raggedy," he says. "They're just thrown together and raggedy, man. After so many years, the steel goes to rust and leaking, commodes stopped up, the plumbing is messed up over the years. This stuff is old."

To solve the violence, Seth believes the ADOC could stop its employees from bringing in drugs and other contraband. He also believes gang members from opposing gangs should be segregated from each other and live with their own.

Asked what he thinks could solve the overcrowding problem, "Start letting folks go and quit locking up so many petty cases," he answers.

* * *

"We've kind of been on lockdown, with the officer getting jumped on, and a search dog got killed or something, sniffing some fentanyl or something like that, and died. They say [an ADOC employee] got stabbed in Ventress," says Cecile when I interview her in early April.

I ask Cecile what solutions she feels would be helpful to the prison system in Alabama or the country in general.

"The overcrowding is the main thing, basically, because by

being so packed in like sardines, it's kind of like it's especially depressing, by us being so overcrowded like we is. I feel like they have to do a mass release or something like that. That would help the prison system more," says Cecile.

"Or," she continues, "the conditions with the food, how they feed the food, or how they prepare the food ... If that was prepared better, I feel like that would help, because our health is one of the main concerns that we try to focus on, trying to survive or stay healthy or whatever while we're in prison."

I ask her to specify what she thinks could solve the overcrowding problems. "A mass release," she suggests. "If they were to approve a mass release right now, that would help. That would be a solution to the overcrowding, because if they release a lot of people, then it'll clear up some space."

I ask what would solve the drug problem. "Wow," she answers, "if the officers just stop bringing it in, man. That's how we're getting it in. The officers are the ones bringing the drugs in. It ain't like we're able to smuggle it in from the outside ... We've got to have some kind of inside source for us to be able to get [the drugs]. If the officers will stop bringing it in, we'll stop doing it. We'll stop having access to it."

Asked what she thinks some solutions could be to discrimination and violence against gay and trans people, she says, "If people would just open their minds up and start understanding that God made everybody in their own unique way and everybody is different, and nobody is the same. Even identical twins, they're not the same. They have some forms of differences about themselves. I just wish people would open up their minds and start seeing that trans-like human beings are just like straight-like human beings. I wish we were all people. You know what I'm saying? We're supposed to be unified and be together, but that's not the case. I just feel like people need to learn how to go out there and live their own life, and just try to open up their eyes instead of being blind to the uniqueness of others being gay or trans. You know what I'm saying? We're different, but we're all people."

I ask Cecile how she thinks the prison system has been handled up to this point, and how she thinks Governor Ivey has handled the crisis. "She's as stubborn as she can be. I'm not saying it's her old age, but she needs to get up off of that stubbornness, because you know everybody deserves a second chance."

Cecile says that Ivey's belief about the prison system is simply, "If you were given the time, you've got to do it." But, she points out, "That's what they made the parole board for, for us to rehabilitate ourselves and try to better ourselves, take programs and classes and trades, and try to elevate ourselves to a point where we are fit for society and we can cope with society once we get back out there. But she's got to open up her mind, too, though. Like, just because we committed a crime, that don't make us less of a human being. That don't make us less of a people. We deserve a second chance like everybody else, man. Everybody deserves a second chance."

* * *

When I interview Nick again, he reiterates what others have said about officers being attacked at multiple prisons in recent weeks, including an officer who was beat up in Bullock, who Nick says has been off work for a couple weeks as of this interview.

"About a week and a half or two weeks ago, they had us on lockdown, but we stay locked down all the time anyway," says Nick.

Reflecting on the time since he has been in Bullock, Nick explains that "I was in D dorm when I got here. I stayed there for about four or five months. Then I moved to F dorm, stayed in there about two months. I moved to E dorm, stayed in there a couple of months. Then I moved over into the I dorm. This is the mental health dorm. This is the only dorm where, when they call a store draw, they won't let all the inmates go to the gym. A lot of guys be wanting to go there and get haircuts and stuff like that, and they ain't able to get up there.

"And they done moved a couple of guys out of here too. I don't know what's going on. I don't know what they done got into, but the lieutenant moved one out yesterday, and the warden moved one out yesterday morning, but he never did leave. [The prisoner] hasn't left yet," he adds.

I ask Nick what he thinks might be some solutions to the problems with the prison system in Alabama or the country in general.

"Well, I feel like just letting a lot of these guys go up out of here, that'll solve it, because it's just too overcrowded, for real," he answers. "Everybody knows everybody's business. Everybody knows what's going on with everybody. And a lot of guys just try to keep things a secret. You know what I mean? But I feel like it's just overcrowded."

Asked what he means about people keeping secrets, Nick explains, "A lot of these guys wind up doing things they don't want people to know, like having sex with other men and doing all these different drugs and owing other people, but people just sit and watch people all day long in here, in this dorm. You can see anything ... But, yeah, the overcrowding is a big part of this Alabama prison system."

Nick elaborates on how he feels the overcrowding problem could be reduced:

"Well," he says, "there are a lot of guys here, man, that have been here 25 and 30 years. What could you have been doing that bad, to be locked up 30, 40 years? I met a guy—if his name is still in the system—his name is Leroy Smith. Leroy Smith got locked up [in] 1973. I was born in 1972 ... I was 44 years old [when I met him]. He had been locked up just that long. I'm 52 years old now. When I left Bibb County, he was still there."

Leroy Smith is indeed still in Bibb Prison in Brent, Alabama. He has been in prison for 52 years.

"What could a man have did to be locked up 50 years, man?" asks Nick. "He got locked up when he was 18 or 19 years old. I've met a lot of guys in prison who got locked up from 14 to 19 years old, and they haven't been out yet. And a lot of them are 55, 60 years old."

He continues, "And I can see a lot of change in these guys, and just being around them over the years, the way they move, the way they act, everything, the way they treat other people."

Another problem that has been bothering Nick and could be fixed is that "a lot of times, the officers, man, they'll talk to you like they're crazy. They cuss at you. They fluff at you. They call you names. They're so unprofessional around here, it ain't real, man."

\* \* \*

Meanwhile, out in the free world, "From I've been seeing on the news," Nick says, "Donald Trump is going to cut Social Security and Disability out beneath us. That's going to be hard on a lot of people that are in prison, because a lot of guys I know in prison, they wait on the first of the month for their people to send them money so that they can get some of their odds and ends, get commissary and stuff like that. If they're cutting that out, man, it's going to be real worse than what it is around here."

\* \* \*

To solve the drug problem, Nick believes that if the administration "could stop the officers from bringing drugs in, it'll stop a lot of these overdoses, because we can't go over the fence and get it."

\* \* \*

"They're supposed to be shutting one of these dorms down here," says Chris when I interview him again in early April. "The sewage is backing up in the kitchen. They're supposed to make a portable kitchen out of one of these dorms, and they're going to transfer everybody [in whichever dorm is chosen], and we don't know what dorm yet."

Chris just heard about it himself not long before this interview. At least the temperature outside has finally warmed up a little, so the prison isn't as cold as it has been, he tells me. He and multiple other prisoners also say an employee was recently busted for bringing drugs into the prison.

\* \* \*

I interview Nick again in early April.

"Our dorm rep went to a dorm rep meeting yesterday, and they're fitting to close the chow hall down here in Bullock," he tells me at the beginning of the conversation. "They don't know which dorm they're going to pick to make the chow hall, but if they choose the dorm that we're in, they're going to transfer everybody that's in the dorm. So, we won't know until a week or two later. You know what I mean?

"But, they're supposed to close the chow hall down and—I don't know if they can—make one of these dorms the chow hall until they ... They're going to redo the chow hall, is my understanding, and whatever dorm they pick, they're going to transfer everybody to another camp. I ain't ever heard of nothing like that. You know what I mean? The chow hall is real small though. You feel me? And they weren't too smart when they built it, for real."

I ask how this might affect him and other prisoners. "Believe it or not, I hope they pick this dorm, because I'm ready to leave here anyway. We're locked down all day. This is an inside camp. We hardly ever get to go outside. But I hope they choose this dorm, so I can get away from here. A lot of us want to get away from here, for real," he answers.

"But," he adds, "I'll still have your number, and I can let you know what's going on at any camp. Matter of fact, I've got it in my head. Derek too, he got [your number] in his head."

\* \* \*

"They're trying to change one of the dorms into a chow hall, something going on with the chow hall. I don't know if it's some kind of malfunction or what, if they failed some kind of inspection or what, but they said they have to move the chow hall into one of these dorms, so they're going to have to transfer everybody out of the dorm to another facility for bed space," says Cecile when I interview her again in April.

I ask what the impact of that is on the prisoners. "That impact is messed up, for real," she answers, "because we done already got settled in. Some of us are settled in, and we really don't feel like moving right now, and we're kind of alright where we're at, so we don't really want to relocate, because you've got to find a whole new setting, got to get into a whole new mode of things. It's a whole new vibe. You've got to go through the reprocessing part."

This could also make the overcrowding problems even worse, since they probably won't have prisoners sleeping in the new chow hall or the old one. Furthermore, if they don't transfer a large number of prisoners, and instead simply spread them out into other dorms throughout Bullock, that will also make the overcrowding worse.

Also, at the time of this interview, "They're still running the [old] kitchen after they done found roaches and rats. Like I said, they probably failed the inspection, or there was some kind of malfunction inside the kitchen ... something going on where they're having to move the kitchen out of the dining hall into one of these dorms and transfer everybody that's in that particular dorm," says Cecile, adding, "We're going to keep you family. Even if we get moved, we've got your number, man. We'll stay in touch with you, and we'll keep you posted on what's going on ... inside the prison."

Cecile says she has my number memorized. Toward the end of the conversation, she calls Seth over to ask if he has my number memorized as well, and they both recite my number back to me, one from the background and one into the phone.

"We got it, man. We're going to keep you posted," says Cecile.

She says they won't know if or where they've been transferred for a couple of weeks.

The Alabama Department of Corrections again did not respond to my request for comment on various aspects of this chapter.

* * *

"Pretty much the same," says Seth when I interview him again in April, "prison being prison. They came in and fixed the hot water. Up in here, you've got to stay to yourself, stay in your lane, because if not, trouble will come find you in here, man."

Despite fixing the hot water, "They said the kitchen didn't pass inspection," Seth says. "I don't know what it was, rats or roaches or what, because we've got roaches really bad in our dorm, so I'm thinking that's probably what it was, rats and roaches in that kitchen when they came through here."

He adds, "They're supposed to be making one of these dorms a kitchen dorm, and putting a portable kitchen outside in the back or something, but they said that everybody in the dorm that they choose is going to be transferred out to other facilities, but we will keep in touch. We're going to basically make you like part of our family, Matt, whether you know it or not, man ... We're going to keep you posted on the inside view of everything going on in here, man. That way, you get it from the horse's mouth instead of just assuming, having the inmates in the stories and the articles that you put out, the full-fledged truth."

# Endnotes

1. Alexander Willis, "Assaults within Alabama Prisons Increase in May, Still Down From Last Year," *Alabama Daily News*, August 6, 2024.

2. Alabama Department of Corrections, "Bullock." https://doc. alabama.gov/facility.aspx?loc=4

3. Bryan Lyman, "Alabama Cannot Build its Way Out of The Prison Crisis," *Alabama Reflector*, April 29, 2024.

4. Matthew Vernon Whalan, "It's Like They're Trying to Kill Us," *Scheer Post*, July 16, 2020.

5. Devlin Barret, "'Cruel and Unusual': Alabama Prisons Plagued by Severe Violence, Justice Dept. Investigation Finds," *Washington Post*, April 3, 2019.

6. Sarah Whites-Koditschek, "Alabama Inmates' HIV Rates Triple Rest of Population," *AL.com*, June 19, 2023.

7. United States District Court Northern District of Alabama in RE: CV-76-P-775-W, Transcript of Proceedings, August 6, 1997, Before the Honorable Sam C. Pointer, Jr. United States District Judge.

8. Southern Poverty Law Center, "SPLC Files Motion to Hold Alabama Accountable for Inadequate Health Care of All State Prisoners," *Southern Poverty Law Center*, August 20, 2016. See also: Julia Marnin, "Inmate Needed an

Endnotes pages 16–39

Amputation After Medical Needs Ignored, Suit Says. Doctor Owes $400k," *Miami Herald*, May 24, 2024.

9. Alabama Department of Corrections, Administrative Regulation 604, *Confidentiality in Mental Health Services.* https://doc.alabama.gov/docs/AdminRegs/AR604.pdf

10. Mike Cason, "Inmate Video Gives Peek Inside Alabama Prison During Quarantine," *AL.com*, August 18, 2020. I've also documented similar issues in Fountain Prison here: Matthew Vernon Whalan, "Fountain Prison, Alabama: Overcrowding, Prisoners Sleeping on Floor, Violence, Heat, Illness, Sewage Leaking From Bathroom Area Into Prison," *Hard Times Reviewer*, July 19, 2024.

11. Matthew Vernon Whalan, "Rats, Cats, and Roaches," *Hard Times Reviewer*, October 31, 2022.

12. Bryan Henry, "Bullock County Leaders in Uncharted Waters Amid Potential Prison Close," *WSFA-12*, February 15, 2019.

13. See one of many pieces I've written this topic here: Matthew Vernon Whalan, "Reflections on Childhood, Grief, and Family After Leaving Alabama Prison," *Hard Times Reviewer*, October 27, 2024.

14. Pugh v. Locke, 406 F. Supp. 318 (M.D. Ala. 1976), https://law.justia.com/cases/federal/district-courts/FSupp/406/318/2143390/

15. Larry W. Yackle, *Reform and Regret: The Story of Federal Judicial Involvement in the Alabama Prison System* (New York: Oxford University Press, 1989), 9–10.

16. Liz Vinson, "'For Cruelty's Sake': State of Alabama Diverts $400 Million in COVID Funds to Build Prisons, Leaving

158

Many in Dire Straits," *Southern Poverty Law Center*, July 1, 2022.

17. Ivana Hrynkiw and Ramsey Archibald, "Alabama's Billion Dollar Prison Plan Does Not End The Overcrowding," *AL.com*, April 7, 2023.

18. Yackle, *Reform and Regret*, 45.

19. "Record Death in Alabama Prisons; Many Were Preventable," Equal Justice Initiative, December 9, 2022.

20. Matthew Vernon Whalan, "Notes on Larry W. Yackle's 1989 Book on Federal Judicial Involvement In Alabama's Prison System From Early 70s to Early 80s: Two Interesting Passages to Think About Today," *Hard Times Reviewer*, October 5, 2024. See Eddie Burkhalter, "Record Loss Of Life in 2023 Pushes ADOC's Death Total Over 1,000 Since DOJ Put State on Notice," *Alabama Appleseed*, January 29, 2024; Eddie Burkhalter, "Death Toll Inside Alabama Prisons Reaches 277 in 2024," *Alabama Appleseed*, January 13, 2025.

21. Ralph Chapoco, "Report: 16% of Bills in 2023 Alabama Legislative Session Could Increase Prison Overcrowding," *Alabama Reflector*, December 6, 2023.

22. Beth Shelburne, "A Parole Board Against Paroles: Who's Behind Alabama's Cold War Against Second Chances?" *Moth to Flame*, August 21, 2022.

23. Ibid.

24. Matthew Vernon Whalan, "Board of Pardons and Paroles and Prison System in Alabama 'Rips Families Apart ... Rips Communities Apart': Part Three in the Oral History Series With Veteran Journalist Eddie Burkhalter on Alabama Prisons," *Hard Times Reviewer*, November 30, 2024.

25. Yackle, *Reform and Regret*, 259.

26. Ibid., 255.

27. Ibid., 212.

28. Ibid., 213.

29. Ibid.

30. Ibid., 242.

31. Ibid., 251.

32. Ibid., 251–52.

33. Ray Downs, "This Small Prison in Rural Alabama is One of The Most Violent Places in America," *Vice*, June 23, 2014.

34. Campbell Robertson, "An Alabama Prison System's Unrelenting Dissent Into Violence," *New York Times*, March 28, 2017.

35. Alabama Department of Corrections, "Statistical Reports," https://doc.alabama.gov/statreports.aspx

36. Matthew Vernon Whalan, "Former ADOC Officer: 'I Had Become Abusive': Part Two in The Oral History Series With Former Alabama Department of Corrections Officer Cedric Long," *Hard Times Reviewer*, March 29, 2025.

37. United States Drug Enforcement Administration, "Flakka (alpha-PVP)," https://www.dea.gov/factsheets/flakka-alpha-pvp

38. DEA TOX, "Announcement of a Newly Identified Synthetic Cannabinoid 4CN-AB-BUTICA," February 25, 2021, https://www.deadiversion.usdoj.gov/dea_tox/4CN-AB-BUTICA.pdf

39. *WSFA 12* Staff, "2 More Inmates Die at Bullock Correctional Facility," *WSFA 12*, May 3, 2024.

40. Alabama Appleseed Center for Law and Justice, *A Bitter Pill: Prisons Have Become The Deadly Epicenter of Alabama's Addiction Crisis, Even as the State's Response Begins to Show*

*Signs of Success Elsewhere* (Montgomery, AL: Alabama Appleseed, 2022), 3.

41. Debbie Elliot, "DOJ: Alabama Prisons For Men Are Unconstitutional Because Staff Abuse Inmates," *NPR*, July 23, 2020.

42. Debbie Elliot, "Justice Dept. Finds Violence in Alabama Prisons 'Common, Cruel, Pervasive,'" *NPR*, April 3, 2019.

43. See Jennifer Gonnerman, "Million Dollar Blocks: The Neighborhood Costs of America's Prison Boom," and Wil S. Hylton, "Sick on the Inside: Correctional HMOs and the Coming Prison Plague," both in: Tara Herivel and Paul Wright, eds., *Prison Profiteers: Who Makes Money From Mass Incarceration* (New York: The New Press, 2007).

44. Ernest Drucker, *A Plague of Prisons: The Epidemiology of Mass Incarceration in America* (New York: The New Press, 2011), 117.

45. Ibid., 124.

46. Ibid., 125.

47. Rebekah J. Stewart, et al., "Tuberculosis Outbreaks in State Prisons, United States, 2011-2019," *American Journal of Public Health*, July 13, 2022, https://pmc.ncbi.nlm.nih.gov/articles/PMC9342802/#:~:text=Seven%20states%20had%20a%20median,%2C%20and%20Texas%20(14.0)

48. Alabama Public Radio, "Prison Reform: Healthcare in Alabama's Prisons," April 29, 2019; Brianna Hollis, "26 Inmates Diagnosed With Scabies at Holman Prison in Atmore," *WKRG 5*, August 12, 2019.

49. Sarah Whites-Koditschek, "Alabama Inmates' HIV Rates Triple Rest of Population," *AL.com*, July 19, 2023.

50. Alabama Department of Public Health, "Hepatitis C and Incarceration," https://www.alabamapublichealth.gov/hepatitis/assets/hep-c-incarceration.pdf

51. Anna Flag, Jamiles Lartey, and Shannon Heffernan, "Officials Failed to Act When COVID Hit Prisons. A New Study Shows The Deadly Cost: People Died in Prison at 3.4 Times The Rate of The Free Population, With The Oldest Hit Hardest. New Data Holds Lesson For Preventing Future Deaths," *The Marshall Project*, April 18, 2024.

52. Alabama Appleseed Center for Law and Justice, *A Bitter Pill.*

53. Eddie Burkhalter, "Fentanyl is Killing People Inside Alabama's Largest, Most Expensive Law Enforcement Agency—The Alabama Department of Corrections," *Alabama Appleseed*, August 14, 2024.

54. NWS Birmingham, Alabama Weather Forecast Office, "Snowfall on January 21, 2025," *National Weather Service*, January 21, 2025.

55. Beth Shelburne, "The Pain and Suffering of Incarceration in Alabama," ALCU Smart Justice Alabama (website) October 25, 2024, https://www.alabamasmartjustice.org/stories/the-pain-and-suffering-of-incarceration-in-alabama

56. David Keech, "State-by-State Ranking: Highest and Lowest Prison Staff Levels in America," *On Focus News*, August 17, 2024.

57. Alabama Department of Corrections, *Monthly Statistical Report for November 2024* (Montgomery: AL: Alabama Department of Corrections, 2024), https://doc.alabama.gov/docs/MonthlyRpts/November%202024.pdf

58. Bryan Lyman, "Alabama Can't Build Its Way Out of The Prison Crisis," *Alabama Reflector*, April 29, 2024.

59. Kimberly Randall, "Policy Watch: Alabama Prison Expansion and the Subsequent Impact on Public Health," University of Alabama at Birmingham Lister Hill Center for Health Policy School of Public Health, October 4, 2021.

60. Prison Policy Initiative, "Alabama Profile," https://www.prisonpolicy.org/profiles/AL.html

61. Eddie Burkhalter, "Fentanyl is Killing People Inside Alabama's Largest, Most Expensive Law Enforcement Agency—The Alabama Department of Corrections," *Alabama Appleseed*, August 14, 2024.

62. Pugh v. Locke, 406 F. Supp. 318 (M.D. Ala. 1976), https://law.justia.com/cases/federal/district-courts/FSupp/406/318/2143390/ ; for more on the history of this practice, see also Ray March, *Alabama Bound : Forty-Five Years Inside a Prison System* (Tuscaloosa: University of Alabama Press, 1978), and Larry W. Yackle, *Reform and Regret: The Story of Federal Judicial Involvement in the Alabama Prison System* (New York: Oxford University Press, 1989).

63. Kim Kelly, "Lawsuit: Alabama is Denying Prisoners Parole to Lease Their Labor to Meatpackers and McDonald's," *In These Times*, April 19, 2024.

64. Tom Gordon, "550 Alabama Inmates Moved Out of Bullock County Prison While Officials Work to Fully Restore Heat and Hot Water," *AL.com*, January 5, 2010.

65. Shelby Bark, "Moving Inmates From Cold Prison Cost ADOC $132k," *The News Courier*, January 15, 2010.

66. United States Department of Justice Civil Rights Division, United States Attorneys Office for the Northern, Middle, and Southern Districts of Alabama, *Investigation of Alabama's State Prisons for Men* (April 2, 2019), 52.

67. Melissa Brown and Bryan Lyman, "Alabama to Close Most of Holman Prison, Move Inmates Across State," *The Montgomery Advertiser*, January 29, 2020.

68. Mike Cason, "Alabama Moving 600 Inmates From Crowded, Dangerous, Deteriorating Holman Prison," *AL.com*, January 29, 2020.

69. Human Rights Watch, *World Report 2017* (New York: Seven Stories Press, 2017), 635.

## About the Author

MATTHEW VERNON WHALAN IS a writer and oral historian living in New England. His work has appeared in *Counterpunch Magazine*, *Alabama Political Reporter*, *Scheer Post*, *Jacobin*, *Eunoia Review*, *New York Journal of Books*, *The Brattleboro Reformer*, and elsewhere. He runs the publication *Hard Times Reviewer* at hardtimesreviewer.substack.com.

Divided World Divided Class: Global Political Economy
and the Stratification of Labour Under Capitalism, SECOND EDITION
Zak Cope • 9781894946681 • 460 pages • $24.95
*Charting the history of the "labour aristocracy" in the capitalist world system, from its roots in colonialism to its birth and eventual maturation into a full-fledged middle class in the age of imperialism. This second edition includes new material such as data on growing inequality between the richest and poorest countries, responses to critiques surrounding the thesis of mass embourgeoisement through imperialism, and more. (2015)*

False Nationalism False Internationalism
E. Tani and K. Sera • 9781989701089 • 341 pages • $30.00
*A critical history of revisionism, opportunism, and parasitical relationships between white and Black revolutionary organizations in the United States. This essay was an attempt to evaluate the rise in radical armed activity in the US during the 1960s and 1970s from an activist perspective. (1985/2021)*

Female Keep Separate & the Hot Tray Hooper:
Jail Life, Gender & the Violence of Inclusion
Rabbit • 9781989701409 • 53 pages • 17.00
*Two powerful texts by anarchist writer Rabbit, reflecting on her experiences of incarceration in Canada and the gendered violence of the prison system. The first, The Hot Tray Hooper, recounts the survival strategies and social codes within a men's provincial jail, drawn with literary attention to the messy reality of life inside. The second, Female Keep Separate, critiques trans liberalism and prison reform, arguing that gender-affirming policies like Ontario's Bill C-16 can deepen carceral control rather than offering liberation, urging abolitionists to reject inclusion into oppressive systems. (2025)*

From Hash Rebels to Urban Guerrillas:
A Documentary History of the 2nd of June Movement
Gabriel Kuhn & Roman Danyluk (eds.) • 9798887440613 • 480 pages • $29.95
*The first book to present the 2nd of June Movement in English, documenting the group's history and politics through translations of original documents and reflections by former members. (2024)*

Ingrid Schubert: Letters from Prison, 1970–1977
Ingrid Schubert • 9798887441085 • 256 pages • $24.95
*Ingrid was one of the first members of the Red Army Faction in West Germany, and was among the first to be imprisoned. This volume contains original letters from prison to her sister, showing her efforts to maintain her integrity, political identity, and at the same time a meaningful exchange with her family. These letters reveal the daily struggle of a political prisoner resisting repression. (2025)*

Jailbreak Out of History: the Re-Biography of Harriet Tubman, SECOND EDITION
Butch Lee • 9781894946704 • 169 pages • $14.95
*Examining how the anticolonial struggles of New Afrikan/Black women were central to the unfolding of 19th-century amerika, both during and "after" slavery. The book's title essay, "The Re-Biography of Harriet Tubman", recounts the life and politics of Harriet Tubman, who waged and eventually led the war against the capitalist slave system. "The Evil of Female Loaferism" details New Afrikan women's attempts to withdraw from and evade capitalist colonialism, an unofficial but massive labor strike which threw the capitalists North and South into a panic. The ruling class response consisted of the "Black Codes", Jim Crow, re-enslavement through prison labor, mass violence, and … the establishment of a neo-colonial Black patriarchy, whose task was to make New Afrikan women subordinate to New Afrikan men just as New Afrika was supposed to be subordinate to white amerika. (2015)*

Looking at the U.S. White Working Class Historically
David Gilbert • 9781894946919 • 97 pages • $10.00
*Examining the contradiction embodied in the term "white working class." On the one hand there is the class designation that should imply, along with all other workers of the world, a fundamental role in the overthrow of capitalism. On the other hand, there is the identification of being part of a ("white") oppressor nation. Gilbert seeks to understand the origins of this contradiction, its historical development, as well as possibilities to weaken and ultimately transform the situation. In other words, how can people organize a break with white supremacy and foster solidarity with the struggles of people of color, both within the United States and around the world? (2017)*

Manufacturing Threats: Case Studies of State Manipulation
and Entrapment in Canada
Alexandre Popovic • 9781989701249 • 292 pages • $20.00
*Telling the story of police provocateurs going back to the time of Canadian Confederation. This book is an important introduction to the subject of Canada's repressive agencies and the legislation and lack of oversight that have structured their use of agents provocateurs and informants over the years. (2022)*

Meditations on Frantz Fanon's Wretched of the Earth:
New Afrikan Revolutionary Writings
James Yaki Sayles • 9781894946322 • 399 pages • $20.00
*One of those who eagerly picked up Fanon in the 1960s, who carried out armed expropriations and violence against white settlers, Sayles reveals how behind the image of Fanon as race thinker there is an underlying reality of antiracist communist thought. "This exercise is about more than our desire to read and understand Wretched (as if it were about some abstract world, and not our own); it's about more than our need to understand (the failures of) the anti-colonial struggles on the African continent. This exercise is also about us, and about some of the things that We need to understand and to change in ourselves and our world." James Yaki Sayles (Atiba Shanna) (2010)*

Night-Vision: Illuminating War and Class on the Neo-Colonial Terrain, SECOND EDITION
Butch Lee and Red Rover • 9781894946889 • 264 pages • $17.95
*bell hooks: "Night-Vision was so compelling to me because it has a spirit of militancy which reformist feminism tries to kill because militant feminism is seen as a threat to the liberal bourgeois feminism that just wants to be equal with men. It has that raw, unmediated truth-telling which I think we are going to need in order to deal with the fascism that's upon us." A foundational analysis of post-modern capitalism, the decline of u.s. hegemony, and the need for a revolutionary movement of the oppressed to overthrow it all. (1998/2017)*

Panther Vision: Essential Party Writings and Art of Kevin "Rashid" Johnson
Kevin "Rashid" Johnson • 978-1-894946-76-6 • 496 pages • $22.95
*A major collection of essays outlining the vision and ideological core of the Revolutionary Intercommunal Black Panther Party, exposing the racist underpinnings of U.S. capitalism, and arguing for the need for a Marxist-Leninist party to resist and overthrow oppression. (2015)*

The Principal Contradiction
Torkil Lauesen • 9781989701034 • 157 pages • $17.00
*An introduction to the philosophy of dialectical materialism as a tool for changing the world. Identifying the principal contradiction is indispensable for developing a global perspective on capitalism. This methodology is not just a valuable tool with which to analyze complex relationships: it also tells us how to intervene. (2020)*

Remembering the Armed Struggle: My Time with the Red Army Faction
Margrit Schiller • 9781629638737 • 256 pages • $20.00
*Schiller recounts the process through which she joined her generation's revolt in the 1960s, going from work with drug users to joining the antipsychiatry political organization the Socialist Patients' Collective and then the RAF. She tells of how she met and worked alongside the group's founding members, Ulrike Meinhof, Andreas Baader, Jan-Carl Raspe, Irmgard Möller, and Holger Meins; how she learned the details of the May Offensive and other actions while in her prison cell; about the struggles to defend human dignity in the most degraded of environments, and the relationships she forged with other women in prison. (2021)*

Settlers: The Mythology of the White Proletariat from Mayflower to Modern
J. Sakai • 9781629630373 • 456 pages • $20.00
*Settlers exposes the fact that America's white citizenry have never supported themselves but have always resorted to exploitation and theft, culminating in acts of genocide to maintain their culture and way of life. As recounted in painful detail by Sakai, the United States has been built on the theft of Indigenous lands and of Afrikan labor, on the robbery of the northern third of Mexico, the colonization of Puerto Rico, and the expropriation of the Asian working class, with each of these crimes being accompanied by violence. This new edition includes "Cash & Genocide: The True Story of Japanese-American Reparations" and an interview with author J. Sakai by Ernesto Aguilar. (2014)*

**The Shape of Things to Come: Selected Writings & Interviews**
J. Sakai • 9781989701218 • 375 pages • $24.95
*Sakai's work is grounded in Mao's politics, anti-imperialism, and in a lifetime of hands-on activism; he has consistently focused on the relationship between "race" and "class" in the american context, from a perspective dedicated to abolishing the united states, capitalism, and white supremacy. Here in this book, for the first time, is presented a selection of writings by Sakai spanning a 40 year period, from 1983 to 2022. This includes three articles initially written anonymously for the anti-imperialist journal S1, and an extensive interview that took place between 2020 and 2022, appearing here for the first time. (2023)*

**A Soldier's Story: Writings by a New Afrikan Anarchist**
Kuwasi Balagoon et al. • 9781629633770 • 272 pages • $21.95
*Kuwasi Balagoon was a participant in the Black Liberation struggle from the 1960s until his death in prison in 1986. A member of the Black Panther Party and defendant in the infamous Panther 21 case, Balagoon went underground. Captured and convicted of various crimes against the State, he spent much of the 1970s in prison, escaping twice. After each escape, he went underground and resumed BLA activity. Balagoon was unusual for his time in several ways. He combined anarchism with Black nationalism, he broke the rules of sexual and political conformity that surrounded him, he took up arms against the white supremacist state—all the while never shying away from developing his own criticisms of the weaknesses within the movements. His eloquent trial statements and political writings, as much as his poetry and excerpts from his prison letters, are all testimony to a sharp and iconoclastic revolutionary who was willing to make hard choices and fully accept the consequences. Balagoon died of AIDS-related pneumonia while in prison in 1986. (2019)*

**The Spirit of Freedom: Anticolonial War & Uneasy Peace in Ireland**
Attack International • 9781989701270 • 115 pages • $12.00
*A powerful and provocative call to the radical left to dig into the Irish republican resistance, "The Spirit of Freedom" has continued to circulate for more than three decades, far beyond the immediate audience at which it was initially aimed, and as the context dramatically shifted. To aid the present-day reader, this edition also includes a new Preface and Afterword by C. Crowle (as well as footnotes and supplements to Attack International's chronology and book recommendations) to update the last thirty years of history of the conflict in the Six Counties of "Northern Ireland." (1989/2023)*

**Stand Up Struggle Forward: New Afrikan Revolutionary Writings on Nation, Class and Patriarchy**
Sanyika Shakur • 9781894946469 • 208 pages • $13.95
*This collection of writings by Sanyika Shakur, formerly known as Monster Kody Scott, includes several essays written from within the infamous Pelican Bay Security Housing Unit in the period around the historic 2011 California prisoners' hunger strike, as well as two interviews conducted just before and after his release in Black August 2012. Firmly rooted in the New Afrikan Communist tradition, he skillfully uses the tools of dialectical materialism to lay bare the deeper connections between racism, sexism, and homophobia and how these mental diseases relate to the ongoing capitalist (neo-) colonial catastrophe we remain trapped within. Stand Up, Struggle Forward also contains a valuable account of political repression in the California prison system, including several of the intelligence memoranda they were used to condemn Shakur to years of solitary confinement in Pelican Bay. These internal prison documents clearly show that this prolonged solitary confinement was a direct result of Shakur's continuing promotion of New Afrikan Revolutionary Nationalist politics. As such, they provide a clear example of the way in which solitary confinement continues to be used as a tool of political repression against thousands of prisoners in California today (2013)*

**The Struggle Within: Prisons, Political Prisoners, and Mass Movements in the United States**
Dan Berger • 9781604869552 • 128 pages • $12.95
*An accessible yet wide-ranging historical primer about how mass imprisonment has been a tool of repression deployed against diverse left-wing social movements over the last fifty years. Berger examines some of the most dynamic social movements across half a century: Black liberation, Puerto Rican independence, Native American sovereignty, Chicano radicalism, white antiracist and working-class mobilizations, pacifist and antinuclear campaigns, and earth liberation and animal rights. (2014)*

**They Never Crushed His Spirit: A Tribute to Richard Williams**
Interfaith Prisoners of Conscience Project (eds.) • 9781894946223 • 142 pages • $17.00
*Richard Williams was a lifelong anti-imperialist and socialist, one of the Ohio 7 convicted in 1984 of having carried out armed actions against racism and imperialism as a member of the United Freedom Front. After over twenty years of captivity and medical neglect, Richard passed away on December 7, 2005, at the age of 58. With an introduction by Lynne Stewart, and contributions by Netdahe Williams Stoddard, Jaan Laaman, Tom Manning, Ray Luc Levasseur, Jamila Levi, Pat Levasseur, Kazi Toure, Mumia Abu-Jamal, Marilyn Buck, Nehanda Abiodun, Sundiata Acoli, Mutulu Shakur, Russell "Maroon" Shoats, Carlos Alberto Torres, Oscar López Rivera, Laura Whitehorn, Susan Rosenberg, Adolfo Matos Antongiorgi, and many other friends, family and comrades. (2005)*

# KER SPL EBE DEB

Since 1998 Kersplebedeb has been an important source of radical literature and agit prop materials.

The project has a non-exclusive focus on anti-patriarchal and anti-imperialist politics, framed within an anticapitalist perspective. A special priority is given to writings regarding armed struggle in the metropole, the continuing struggles of political prisoners and prisoners of war, and the political economy of imperialism.

The Kersplebedeb website presents historical and contemporary writings by revolutionary thinkers from the anarchist and communist traditions.

Kersplebedeb can be contacted at:

Kersplebedeb
CP 63560
CCCP Van Horne
Montreal, Quebec
Canada
H3W 3H8

email: info@kersplebedeb.com
web:　www.kersplebedeb.com
　　　www.leftwingbooks.net

# Kersplebedeb

www.ingramcontent.com/pod-product-compliance
Lightning Source LLC
Chambersburg PA
CBHW052132270326
41930CB00012B/2850